AIR VANGUARD 4

MARTIN B-26 MARAUDER

MARTYN CHORLTON

First published in Great Britain in 2013 by Osprey Publishing,
Midland House, West Way, Botley, Oxford, OX2 0PH, UK
43-01 21st Street, Suite 220B, Long Island City, NY 11101, USA
E-mail: info@ospreypublishing.com

Osprey Publishing is part of the Osprey Group

A CIP catalogue record for this book is available from the British
Library

Print ISBN: 978 1 78096 605 2
PDF ebook ISBN: 978 1 78096 606 9
ePub ebook ISBN: 978 1 78096 607 6

Index by Sharon Redmayne
Typeset in Deca Sans and Sabon
Originated by PDQ Media, Bungay, UK
Printed in China through Asia Pacific Offset Limited

13 14 15 16 17 10 9 8 7 6 5 4 3 2 1

Osprey Publishing is supporting the Woodland Trust, the UK's leading
woodland conservation charity, by funding the dedication of trees.

www.ospreypublishing.com

CONTENTS

MARTIN B-26 MARAUDER

INTRODUCTION

Over the years, many military aircraft have been criticized with the benefit of hindsight and following the creation of a few myths. The B-26 Marauder bucked the trend slightly by suffering a great deal of criticism from the start. Some of it was justified, while negative comments were generally about its very advanced design because traditional rules were being broken and pushed to the limit of known technology. The pressure of an impending world war certainly aggravated the situation and, if development had taken place in peacetime, many of the Marauder's early foibles would have been ironed out months, if not years, before the type entered frontline service.

The challenging handling of the aircraft, especially in inexperienced hands, resulted in many early casualties and this was especially true of the early models during flight training with the 21st BG (Bombardment Group) at MacDill Field, Tampa in Florida. It was not long before the first of many unflattering and unjustified labels were attached to the B-26. These included the exaggerated 'a Marauder a day in Tampa Bay', the equally unflattering 'Martin Murderer' and the 'Widow Maker'. The main cause of these early losses was a lack of primary twin-engined trainers, which resulted in 'green' crews being unleashed on one of the world's most advanced bombers. The lack of wing area was also quickly noted and it was claimed to be displaying 'no visible means of support' which brought about the nicknames of the 'Baltimore Whore' and the 'Flying Prostitute'.

Martin B-25B-25-MA Marauder 41-1788 of the 449th BS, 322nd BG, in company with B-25C-5-MO 41-34763, from the same unit. While the ultimate fate of 41-1788 is unknown, 41-34763 was brought down by Fw 190s between Quittebeuf and Le Neubourg, France on 3 November 1945. All six crew survived to become PoWs. (Via author)

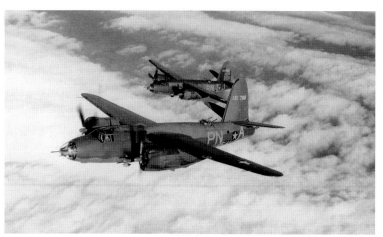

Despite these early problems, which almost saw the USAAF (United States Army Air Force) abandon the B-26 in favour of the vice-free B-25, the Marauder went on to become a success story and rewarded those crews that showed the 'Maligned Madame' the most respect. The B-26 not only proved to be one of the most reliable in its class but also achieved one of the lowest loss rates of a USAAF bomber during World War II.

DESIGN AND DEVELOPMENT

Bomber pioneer

Glenn Luther Martin was one of the early aviation pioneers in the United States, establishing his 'first' Glenn L. Martin Company on 16 August 1912. The young businessman was a self-taught aviator who, by the tender age of 22, owned a Ford and Maxwell dealership in Santa Ana, California. During the early days, Martin kept the fledgling aviation company going by carrying out flying exhibitions and any money he earned would be used to pay his staff and help buy more materials. Martin had no technical knowledge or engineering experience with regard to aircraft other than being able to fly. As such, from the very beginning, Martin employed the most highly trained engineers he could afford and the best managers to run the organization. Many great aviation personalities found their feet working for Martin, including Lawrence Bell, William Boeing (Martin taught Boeing how to fly), Donald Douglas and James S. McDonnell. Other former employees were Charles Day, the senior designer for Standard Aircraft during World War I, and Charles Willard, one of the founding members of the influential LWF (Lowe Willard & Fowler) Engineering Company. Other big names who went on to greater things were J. H. Kindelberger and C. A. Van Dusen, who would lead North American and the Brewster Aircraft Company in the future.

A young Glenn L. Martin, who was one of the United States' great aviation pioneers and creator of an aircraft company that led the way during the immediate post-World War I period. (Via author)

In September 1916, Martin was tempted into a merger with the Wright Company, resulting in the Wright-Martin Aircraft Company. It was an unhappy partnership and, on 10 September 1917, Martin re-formed the Glenn L. Martin Company, based in Cleveland, Ohio, which was destined to remain near the top of the aircraft manufacturing tree for another four decades. Prior to Martin going alone for a second time, the small company had produced 68 different aircraft, the bulk of which were tractor biplanes for training and reconnaissance. This changed from 1918 onwards when Martin began to build bombers for the first time, namely the MB-1, designed by Donald Douglas, of which 20 were ordered by the United States Army Air Service on 17 January 1918. The MB-1 was the first US-built bomber for the US Army but it arrived too late to see any action during World War I and only a handful were built. However, the decision to order the MB-1 was a significant one as, up to this time, aircraft manufacturers and advocates of the bomber had had a tough time convincing the military that there was a role for such an aircraft in a war.

While successful in its own right, the descendant of the MB-1, the MB-2, also referred to as the NBS-1 (Night Bomber, Short Range), received a considerably larger order of 130 aircraft. Unfortunately, only 20 of them were actually built by Glenn L. Martin because the design of the MB-2 was retained by the War Department who tendered out the aircraft to other manufacturers. As a result, 50 MB-2s were built by Curtiss, 35 by LWF Engineering and 25 by Aeromarine. Regardless, Martin had clearly put itself at the forefront of bomber design and the MB-2 became the standard bomber of the US Army Air Service throughout the 1920s. Martin turned the tables on this method of tendering to other manufacturers when in 1925, it won an order for the Curtiss-designed CS-1 and CS-2. Martin redesignated the seaplane the SC-1 and the landplane the SC-2, and won an order for 75 aircraft. By 1929, Glenn L. Martin had sold its Cleveland factory and moved to a brand-new plant at Middle River, Maryland, on the north-eastern side of Baltimore.

Designed by Donald Douglas, who in his own right would create another of the United States' great aircraft manufacturers, the Martin MB-1 was the company's first serious and moderately successful bomber aircraft. (Via author)

The 1930s saw Martin diversify into military and civilian flying boats but, once again, the company's biggest success came with the design of another bomber. The Martin B-10 was the world's first all-metal monoplane, which entered service with the US Army Air Corps (USAAC) in June 1934. The B-10 introduced a host of revolutionary new design features including enclosed cockpits, a retractable undercarriage and revolving gun turrets. As with the MB-2 before it, the B-10 became the mainstay of the USAAC bomber inventory and by the end of production 342, including several sub-variants, had been built. The B-10 also propelled Martin onto the world market and aircraft were exported to Argentina, China, the Dutch East Indies, Indonesia, the Philippines, Siam, Turkey and the Soviet Union. As good as it was, other manufacturers were developing advanced bombers at a tremendous rate during the mid-1930s and the success of the B-10 was overshadowed when the Boeing B-17 and the Douglas B-18 arrived on the scene.

A new bomber for the Army Air Corps

During the mid-1930s, the USAAC was dependent on the B-10 and the B-18 in the medium bomber role. Neither compared to what was being built in Europe with regard to their performance, bomb load or defensive armament. In January 1939, the Army Air Corps issued an outlined proposal for a brand-new medium bomber. All the major US aircraft manufacturers received the request and Douglas, Stearman, North American and Martin all set to work on new designs. The exact specification for a twin-engined medium bomber under 'Circular Proposal' No.39-640 was issued on 11 March 1939.

The proposal was brought into being following the return of Charles Lindbergh from a visit to Germany. Whilst there, Lindbergh witnessed how advanced the Luftwaffe had become and how far behind US military aviation was. No.39-640 requested an aircraft capable of over 300mph, with a range of up to 2,000 miles and, most importantly, the ability to carry 3,000lb of bombs. The emphasis on the new bomber's speed at first outweighed all others and, during a visit to Wright Field, the source of the proposal, Martin's chief engineer and test pilot William E. 'Ken' Ebel had this point stressed to him personally.

To achieve these figures it had already been accepted by the Army Air Corps that the design would have a high wing loading, high landing speed and a long take-off run. Crucially, no stalling speed was specified, an important fact that the chief designer Peyton M. Magruder latched onto. A figure of 97mph with full flaps was later chosen, a figure that was partially psychological in that it did not sound as fast as 100mph! On top of this, the new bomber was to have sufficient defensive armament, armour for the crew, self-sealing fuel tanks, and the wing tip had to be visible from the pilot's seat to make taxying easier.

The Type 179 is born

On 5 July 1939, Martin submitted its bid for their new Model 179, which was broken down into 15 proposals, mainly made up of different engine types and supercharger combinations. Of the 15, six proposed an aircraft powered by the Pratt & Whitney R-2800, five the Wright (WAC) 2600 and four for the WAC R-3350; all of these engines were still under development. The size of the wing was one of the most contentious points of Martin's proposal, with the company suggesting a wing of 650sq ft, which would only be adopted at a much later stage. After much deliberation, Martin's Proposal No.6 won the day, a design that would make use of a pair of Pratt & Whitney R-2800 engines fitted with single-stage, twin-speed superchargers and a wing of just 600sq ft. Behind the scenes Magruder had actually wanted Proposal No.14 which used the WAC R-3350, and a provisional design was also laid down for when this unit became available. The R-3350 came too late for the B-26 but arrived in time for the B-29.

'Ken' Ebel gently eases back on the control column to lift the first production B-26 40-1361 into the air on 25 November 1940. Ebel, who was 41 years old, was a talented aeronautical engineer as well as test pilot. (Via author)

Sophisticated and unique

Initially, the Type 179 adopted the traditional twin-tail arrangement of the day but after extensive wind tunnel testing, it was discovered that a single tail was just as effective and gave the rear gunner a better field of fire. Both electrical and hydraulic systems, which had not been fully exploited before, were another novel feature of the Type 179, although these systems would be the bane of many a ground engineer's life in the future. The Martin bomber, as was becoming traditional with the company, introduced a host of new features, including the use of large alloy castings for the first time, emergency air brakes, very strong clear plastic mouldings, self-sealing fuel tanks and a power-operated gun turret.

The final Type 179 became the first of nine different fighters and bombers to use the new R-2800 engine fitted with a Curtiss electric propeller. The strong fuselage was a monocoque design with a flush-riveted Alclad skin and internally, the majority of the structure was spot-welded. To remove wrinkles from the skin of the Type 179, the fuselage was baked to make the surface finish as perfect as possible, to avoid reducing the potential top speed of the aircraft.

Proposal 39-640 used a scoring system to choose the best candidate. The potential maximum score was 1,000 points and Martin won over its nearest rival, North American, by 140 points. The US Army Air Corps wanted 385 new medium bombers but, thanks to orders that were already in place for the Maryland and the Baltimore aircraft for the RAF and French Air Force, Martin could not commit to the full order. As a result, the Army Air Corps split its order for the medium bomber by ordering 201 Type 179s (designated B-26 by the Army) and 184 North American NA-62s (designated B-25).

While credit for the design of the B-26 Marauder has been firmly placed at the feet of 'project engineer' Peyton M. Magruder, this son of a US Army brigadier general was part of a much larger team of engineers and designers, all of whom contributed to the design of the bomber. These included the chief engineer Ken Ebel, executive engineer G. T. Willey (later general manager of the Nebraska Plant and vice president of the company), Ivan Driggs, Carl Hartgard, Fred Jewett, Clifford Leisy, James Murray, Clifford Roberts and Larry Wade.

Hurdle jumping

Such an advanced design demanded advanced components, but one of the biggest general problems that Martin and in particular Magruder had to face was trying to find manufacturers to make the new parts. Magruder and his design team worked tirelessly on the design of the B-26 and equally hard finding various companies to take on the work. Just as one hurdle was jumped another problem would inevitably present itself. One of the biggest involved the dorsal turret.

Technicians at Wright Field had contacted Magruder and asked if the B-26's dorsal turret could be replaced by an electric one rather than a hydraulic version, as per the original design. Many problems had already been encountered with hydraulic turrets, including fluid leaks and the lack of reliability in cold conditions. Rather than dismissing the idea out of hand, Magruder set about designing an electric one – something that had never been attempted before. Finding motors powerful enough for the job was the initial obstacle, but General Electric stepped up to the parapet and declared that they could produce such a unit. However, it would take the company nine months to make them!

Magruder was having none of it and he was soon on a flight to the General Electric headquarters in Schenectady, New York. It was while flying to New York that he began a conversation with the man sat next to him, telling the stranger all of the problems he was experiencing with General Electric. Remarkably, the stranger in question was the head of General Electric, Charles E. Wilson. This stroke of luck for Magruder and the B-26 project as a whole saw the problem with the production time of the turret motors immediately resolved.

The next hurdle for Magruder concerned the transit of ammunition from a spacious position near the bomb bay to the rear turret. Specialists on the subject said that the machine guns would not be able to pull the ammunition over such a distance, but Magruder thought outside the box and started working on a track system, similar in concept to one used by a toy train. Attention was then turned to one of the country's biggest toy manufacturers, the Lionel Manufacturing Company, New York City. In no time at all an agreement had been reached for Lionel to manufacture the miles of track needed, which would enable B-26 rear gunners to have a supply of 800rpg (rounds per gun), twice as many as available to the rear gunner of a B-17 or B-24.

An electrical system for dropping the bombs was also dismissed by experts, which up until the B-26 was an operation carried out by a complicated collection of rods. Magruder overcame the problem and designed a much neater method of releasing the bombs.

Fuel tanks were another subject that had not evolved for years, entrenched in peacetime thinking. In a combat situation a single hit would not only cause loss of fuel, but was obviously a fire hazard as well. Self-sealing fuel tanks had already been introduced in Britain with the Fairey Battle, but it was not until 1941 that Ernst Eger of the US Rubber Company patented the idea in the United States. Magruder made sure that the B-26 would be the first US military aircraft to use self-sealing tanks and all aircraft designed and built afterwards were fitted with them as standard.

Magruder's 'can do' attitude filtered down through the entire B-26 design team and not a single potential improvement of the design or aircraft during

The 41-year-old Ken Ebel at the controls of the first B-26, 40-1361, in December 1940 not long after its maiden flight. Ebel was an excellent aeronautical engineer and test pilot who had previously failed his advanced training with the USAAC for 'being too conservative', which was unsympathetically officially described as having 'flying deficiencies'. (Via author)

its service life was dismissed. The men involved in the project had tremendous foresight in exactly what was needed to produce an effective warplane. The team's ability to solve the unsolvable, not only in a short space of time but also without the luxury of a prototype to test all their theories, is a tribute to all their professions and undoubtedly made a significant contribution to the outcome of World War II.

Ordered off the drawing board

By late 1939, Europe had already been consumed by war, and despite the United States not being involved at this stage there was an air of inevitability. Events across the Atlantic certainly influenced the War Department's decision to order the B-26 straight from the drawing board, while the B-25 received its order following the development of a single prototype, which was the more traditional 'peacetime' approach. There was no time to order a single prototype from Martin, which would have been hand-built and then put through a host of trials and tests before an order could be placed. On 10 August 1939, the Marauder became the first of many World War II aircraft to be ordered off the drawing board, with contractual approval issued one month later. Orders followed for 139 B-26As fitted with self-sealing tanks and extra armour on 16 September, followed 12 days later by a further 719 B-26Bs. This brought total orders up to 1,131 aircraft, 14 months before the first aircraft was due to fly!

1: B-26 40-1361
The very first Martin B-26 Marauder was not really a prototype, but more like the first production aircraft. Serialed 40-1361, the bomber first flew in the hands of Ken Ebel on 25 November 1940.

2: B-26A (22nd BG, 5th AF)
The B-26A, 40-1424, as flown by 2nd Lt W. S. Watson and crew against Japanese warships off Midway Island on 4 June 1942. This operation was one of the few where the US Army Air Corps deployed Marauders armed with torpedoes.

3: B-26B-4-MO (449th BS, 322nd BG)
The first of two aircraft belonging to the 322nd BG to be named *Impatient Virgin* was B-26B-4-MO, 41-18075. The bomber succumbed to flak over Landrethun-le-Nord, France on 5 November 1943.

4: B-26C-45-MO (443rd BS, 320th BG)
B-26C-45-MO, *Alabama Express* 42-107791, as flown by Lt William J. Cook of the 443rd BS, 320th BG from El Bathan and Djedeida in Tunisia.

An impressive view of B-26 Marauder production in Martin's Omaha, Nebraska plant in 1943. It was located at Fort Crook, later known as Offutt Field. (Via author)

There was an early illustration of the disadvantages of not having a prototype of this advanced aircraft design. Just before Ken Ebel flew the very first B-26 on its maiden flight on November 25, 1940, Ebel realized that he had no experience flying an aircraft with a tricycle undercarriage, let alone a bomber in this configuration! However, the North American B-25 Mitchell had first flown on August 19, 1940 and, to allow him to gain some experience, North American allowed Ebel to fly the aircraft, in secret, from their plant in California. In the end, Ebel's first flight, accompanied by co-pilot Ed Fenimore and flight engineer Al Melwski, was an uneventful one and flight testing of the first production aircraft progressed swiftly, only interrupted by strut failure of the nose undercarriage.

The first four B-26s built were used solely for flight testing and all of them completed a set 133-hour US Army Air Corps test programme. The problem of nose wheel failures would plague the early aircraft, which began to be delivered to US Army Air Corps units from February 1941 – only 23 months after the original specification had been laid down. Not long after its service debut, the B-26 was grounded because of a spate of strut failures, which were later attributed to a manufacturing fault by the sub-contractor producing them. However, the B-26 was very nose-heavy at this stage as it was being flown without a dorsal turret, machine guns or ammunition, which would have taken the weight off the nose wheel.

Inevitably, with such a complex new aircraft, other teething problems would rear their heads during the first few months of service. As with the nose wheel, Martin was let down by components that were not produced by them, such as cracking exhaust sleeves, which was a Pratt & Whitney manufacturing fault. Another dangerous fault, which was later attributed to the sub-contractor trying to cut costs, was the failure of carburettor diaphragms. The inferior material that they were made from was failing at a crucial stage, causing many B-26s to crash on take-off. Once these were re-manufactured in nylon with a rubber cover the problem was cured.

The complex hydraulic system also caused many problems. However, it was not problems with the design, but rather with the ground personnel's lack of training and experience. In the air, where minor faults become considerably more serious, the failure of the Curtiss electric propeller controls did cause several accidents, the majority of them during the critical phases of take-off. The problem was quickly attributed to overuse of electrical systems on the ground, which would run the aircraft's internal batteries down to a dangerous point, resulting in failures of vital equipment during flight when they were most needed. This problem was solved by introducing battery trolleys which the aircraft's many electrical systems could run off, rather than using its own batteries.

Taming the 'hot ship'

Training crews to fly the B-26 became the responsibility of 21st BG at MacDill Field, Tampa. Initially the unit only had a few examples of early production machines, which were watched over by personnel from both Martin and Pratt & Whitney. The aircraft's reputation preceded it and even the qualified B-25 pilots who were selected for conversion treated the aircraft with respect, but still found the Marauder easier than expected to tame. However, for those pilots who had recently graduated from flying school with no twin-engined experience, the B-26 was somewhat daunting. The inevitable early spate of accidents occurred to such a degree that a Board of Inquiry was arranged by the USAAF in 1942.

During one 30-day period, 15 B-26s were written off at MacDill, with many of the incidents incurring casualties. The majority of accidents took place following an engine or propeller failure, and did so with alarming regularity – resulting in the 21st BG declaring that the B-26 could not be landed safely on a single engine. Some trainee pilots even refused to fly the B-26, but this lack of confidence in the bomber was soon turned when several senior test pilots from Wright Field descended upon MacDill to demonstrate how to fly the aircraft safely. Particular emphasis was placed on how to fly the B-26 on one engine and how to land it in this configuration, while extra instruction was given on the correct procedure to feather the Curtiss propellers.

Once mastered the B-26 was a rewarding aircraft to fly, but the damage to its reputation at such an early stage of its career, through gossip and general misinformation, would never be fully shaken off. There is no doubting the B-26 accident rate during 1942 was high at 165 accidents per 100,000 flying hours, compared to the B-25 suffering 104 in the same time. However, for every three B-26s written off, four A-20 Havocs and five P-38 Lightnings were destroyed – and neither of these types ever received the same level of criticism during or after the war, nor were labelled with such gloomy nicknames.

Flying the B-26 was a joy for an experienced professional pilot with many flying hours under his belt. One pilot described the bomber as being 'as manoeuvrable as a P-38 fighter'. This comment was both flattering and a veiled warning – that the B-26 needed the same standard of attention to get the best from it. In the next breath it was described as an aircraft 'you had to stay on top of...'

Although devoid of any markings, this aircraft is most likely B-26A 41-7345, the first of 139 of the variant built, pictured at Middle River on 18 September 1941. This aircraft remained in the US until it was wrecked at Big Springs, Texas on 8 July 1943. (Via author)

By far the most common variant, 1,883 B-26Bs were built, which equated to approximately one-third of all Marauders produced. This aircraft, 41-17876, a B-26B-2-MA, clearly displays the modified engine cowlings that housed sand filters for operations in the MTO (Mediterranean Theatre of Operations). (Via author)

'Automotive' production

Another side-effect of building an aircraft without a prototype was that it would have to be developed while in production; the first significant modification resulted in a new, larger wing and tail surfaces being introduced in an attempt to reduce the high wing loading. This major modification first arrived with the B-26C, which was the first 'automotive' variant and was built at Martin's new Omaha factory at Fort Crook (later Offutt Field) in Nebraska, and the B-26B-10, which was built in Baltimore. 'Automotive' was a term used by the US Army Air Corps for a consortium of manufacturers which, in the B-26's case was Chrysler, Goodyear and Hudson, who produced the aircraft's sub-assemblies and then delivered them to Omaha for assembly by Martin. This method was already working well in practice with the consortium of Boeing, Vega and Douglas, which was successfully producing the B-17. The same could not be said of the B-26 consortium, which lacked experience in aircraft production, and this was complicated by a lack of management co-ordination at the Nebraska factory.

The first B-26Cs, fitted with the larger wing, left the Omaha plant in October 1942. The benefits of the new wing were quickly compounded by increasing the bomber's armour and loading more ammunition on board. By the time the B-26C entered service it had a higher wing loading than the original aircraft.

Improving landing performance

Following a great deal of wind tunnel work, NACA (National Advisory Committee for Aeronautics) suggested several different ways in which landing and take-off performance could be improved. These included wing slots, drooped ailerons, closed undercarriage doors in flight, and even full-span flaps that had the potential to lower the landing speed to just 82mph. Martin took NACA's advice and, one by one, added each modification to a standard B-26 flown by Martin test pilot, Sam Shannon, who had been with the company since 1936.

The day's testing began with a morning flight trial of the standard B-26. In the afternoon, the modification would be fitted and the results of the two flights compared to see if an improvement, or in some cases a deterioration, of the flight envelope had occurred. After several weeks of experimentation, Shannon was to discover that hardly any of the modifications made any improvement to the standard aircraft's take-off or landing performance. In fact, Shannon found that all he had managed to achieve was to improve his own handling of the standard aircraft; for example, at the beginning of the trials he was using up 2,800ft of runway but by the end had shaved 1,000ft off that figure. The real result of the trial was that the only way the handling of the B-26 could be improved was by pilot experience; the more you flew it the better you got to know the bomber.

While Shannon was carrying out his flight trials, a batch of US Army Air Corps flying instructors were sent to Martin for additional training. O. E. 'Pat' Tibbs, who had taken over from Ken Ebel as chief test pilot, was overseeing the course. What Tibbs found astonishing was that the military instructors only had an average total of 350 hours on B-26s, compared to his 5,000 hours! It was a situation where the instructors were not experienced enough to pass their knowledge to the young airmen, who only months earlier had been civilians.

Outgrowing its class

In September 1942, a report issued by the Chief of the Air Service Command, Wright Field, stated that the B-26 was following a trend that would see the aircraft leave the 'class' it was intended for. The report did not hold back in its criticism of a number of areas, including the fact that the aircraft was now to be operated 2,100lb heavier than when it first entered service, which had the knock-on effect of reducing the cruising speed from 250 to 200mph at the same power settings. The lower cruising speed had also been aggravated by an increased positive angle of attack.

A list of recommendations to help improve the performance of the B-26 included several modifications that were carried out following combat

Although it is a B-26B, this aircraft, 42-43459, was used to test the increased incidence wing for the B-26F. While the new wing did have the decided positive effect of shortening the take-off run, it also had the negative effect of reducing the top speed to 277mph at 10,000ft. (Via author)

In total, 1,214 B-26Cs were built. Ninety-nine of them were supplied to the RAF as Marauder IIs, including this one, FB482, which only served with the A&AEE (Aeroplane & Armament Experimental Establishment) and Cunliffe-Owen Aircraft. Note the torpedo shackles in place on the lower fuselage. (Via author)

experience in the Pacific, such as moving the waist gunner's position and removing the ventral gun. Reducing equipment and ammunition on board were also recommended as well as sealing the rear bomb bay and modifying the forward bomb-bay doors to the same design used by the B-24 Liberator, as in a roll-up type. Repositioning of the dorsal turret, which had also been completed on the B-24, to the space originally used by the radio compartment was also recommended and trialled on the sole XB-26E. While the rear bomb-bay doors were later sealed on those aircraft operating in the ETO (European Theatre of Operations), the proposed roll-type doors were never applied to the B-26 due to the complexity of the modification.

Another controversial weight-saving recommendation that came from Air Service Command was the removal of the co-pilot's position. Once the seat, column and cables were removed, the weight saved was almost 3,000lb. A total of 57 B-26C-6-MOs were selected for the conversion but only 49 were actually converted before the complaints began to pour in from operational units (all home-based) which led to all of them being converted back to a two-pilot configuration. Only the 323rd BG, operating in the ETO, was equipped with the single-seaters. It was described by the unit's commanding officer as an aircraft where, 'weight was never a handicap in this aircraft if properly flown'. Once again, it was all down to experience and correct handling by the crew.

It is possible that a ground-attack variant, of which only one B-26B was converted, would have suited being flown by a single pilot. The heavily armed B-26 was test-flown by 'Pat' Tibbs who tested the aircraft's weaponry, which included a 37mm cannon, two extra .50in machine guns in the nose and four more .50in guns in packages either side of the fuselage, against a floating target out at sea. Tibbs described the effect of the rounds hitting the target and the sea as a 'cloud burst' that churned the ocean when he opened up with all guns blazing. The heavy cannon and additional .50in guns were never included on future variants, nor was the idea of a ground-attack variant pursued. The four package guns were retained, not only for defensive purposes but also to strafe targets as and when the opportunity arose.

The final twist

The final and most successful attempt to improve the B-26 had sour beginnings for Martin. The company proposed that the incidence of the wing could be increased by a further 3.5 degrees to help improve handling. The problems began when Glenn Martin, in person, verbally agreed with General Arnold that the work could be carried out. When the USAAF procurement office got to hear of the 'unofficial' modification, they immediately jumped to the wrong conclusion that Martin was trying to pull the wool over their eyes in an attempt to slow the production rate, which would raise the cost of each aircraft. Once the relevant department was officially informed, the work was allowed to be carried out on the proviso that the modification, known as

The last of 5,268 B-26s built was B-26G 44-68254 *Tail End Charlie "30"* which left the Middle River factory in early 1945. It was delivered to the French Air Force on 10 May 1945. The only significant difference between the B-26G and its predecessor was that it was fitted with R-2800-43 engines. (Via author)

the 'twisted wing', would not hinder mainstream production of the bomber. The new wing was received with great enthusiasm by pilots, many going so far as to say that if it had been designed into the original aircraft, considerably fewer crews would have been lost in flying accidents and on operations.

The new wing was built into the final two Marauder variants, the B-26F and G, both of which benefitted from better handling and improved visibility, although the maximum speed was reduced slightly. While production of the B-26F gained momentum at Baltimore, earlier aircraft were enjoying a new lease of life as advanced trainers, designated the AT-23.

The B-26C continued to be produced at the Omaha plant until April 1944 when the last of more than 1,200 examples was rolled out. It was under the control and firm guidance of Joseph T. Hartson, who was put in charge of the plant by Glenn Martin, that the factory was quickly brought up to scratch to become an organized production line. The speed and efficiency of production was increased under Hartson's guidance, only being halted on a single occasion when a B-25, climbing out of the neighboring Offutt Field on a flight test, crashed through the roof of the factory. Three of the crew were killed instantly while a fourth survived, albeit critically injured. The North American bomber actually lodged itself in the roof girders, managing to tear a 75ft-long hole in the roof. As the B-25 burned the ammunition on board began to explode, but despite the carnage only one B-26 (which was directly below) was destroyed and the bulk of the factory workers, all of whom escaped injury, were at lunch outside the factory.

Aircraft production did not come to an end after the B-26. As early as the spring of 1943, it had been decided that the plant would build the B-29 Superfortress; 536 of them would leave with the 'MO' designation.

It was not until April 1945 that the final B-26 was rolled out of the Middle River, Baltimore plant. Named *Tail End Charlie*, the aircraft took off with Pat Tibbs in the pilot's seat and none other than Ken Ebel in the co-pilot's seat. Ebel flew the aircraft for 30 minutes of the two-and-a-half-hour flight, becoming one of only a handful of test pilots to fly both the very first and the very last aircraft built.

TECHNICAL SPECIFICATIONS

A very advanced machine

The B-26 was designed to be flown, at first, by five crew; two pilots, a navigator/bombardier, wireless operator/gunner and an armourer/gunner. The crew later increased to seven and, very often, as many as nine as the war progressed, including specialist equipment operators. All were contained within a semi-monocoque aluminium alloy fuselage made up of three fabricated sections. The fuselage was made up of four main longerons, joined by transverse circular frames and bridged by longitudinal stringers, all covered by a metal skin. The only fabric-covered surface on the whole aircraft was the rudder. The centre section of the fuselage which contained the bomb bay was built integrally into the wing section. The high wing gave the added advantage of a capacious bomb bay that could carry a load of up to 4,800lb; well above the original specification. The wing was relatively short, at just 65ft, and had an area of 602sq ft, which equated to a very high wing loading of 53.2lb/sq ft. Compare this to a Martin B-10, which had a loading of just 21.7lb/sq ft.

From below each wing hung a Pratt & Whitney R-2800-5 Double Wasp radial, each producing 1,850hp, contained within a nacelle. One of the finest aircraft engines ever built, the double-row, 18-cylinder, air-cooled radial had a displacement of 2,804cu in (46 litres). The engine was quite small with a diameter of only 52.8in and a dry weight of just 2,360lb. Because of the R-2800's excellent power to weight ratio, the engine initially posed several challenges on how to keep it cool. The older-style forged cooling fins were not up to the job so a set of bespoke, very thin and carefully shaped fins were produced specifically for the Double Wasp. The engine also introduced a new baffle system to help control the rate and direction of cool air around the engine.

The Double Wasp was fitted with a single-stage, variable speed supercharger and a Stromberg fuel injection carburettor. When the engine was first introduced, the R-2800 had no air-cooled competitors that could equal its power to weight ratio. As with the B-26, the Double Wasp engines were continuously modified and refined and would continue to power the US Air Force through the Korean War period and into the 1960s.

At the rear of each engine nacelle was the main hydraulically actuated undercarriage leg, which was a tricycle arrangement. The nose wheel rotated through 90 degrees and twisted into the horizontal to lay flat, directly below the cockpit floor.

TAIL GUN DIFFERENCES
1. The tail gun position of a B-26A fitted with a single .50in machine gun
2. Redesigned tail gun position of the B-25B fitted with a pair of .50in machine guns
3. Twin .50in machine guns of a hydraulic Bell M-6 or M-6A mount of a B-26B-10
4. A Bell M-6 twin-gun tail 'stinger' as fitted to the B-26B-20, B-26C-10 onwards and the B-26F & B-26G

ENGINE COWLING DIFFERENCES
5. The narrow early engine cowlings of a B-26A fitted with R-2800-5 engines
6. Later, deeper engine cowlings introduced from the B-26B onwards fitted with R-2800-41 engines

TORPEDO DETAILS
7. A 2,000lb 18in torpedo attached to the under-fuselage with a pair of cables, which passed through holes in the closed bomb-bay doors

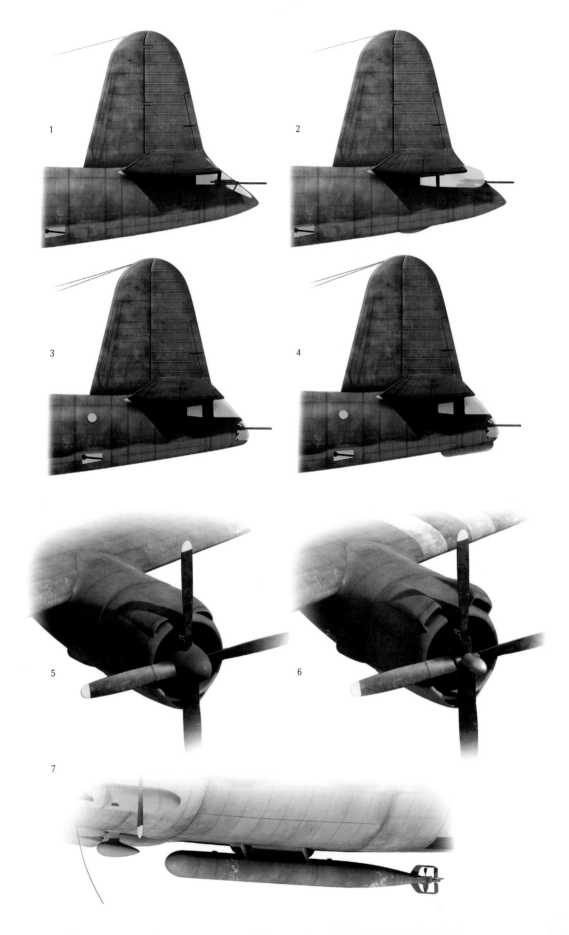

An all-up weight (AUW) of 32,000lb, lack of wing area and high loading all combined to produce some unsurprisingly high performance figures throughout the envelope. A top speed of 315mph (362kts) was attainable but this came at the price of a high landing speed of 130mph (150kts) and only half of the original range requirement could be achieved.

Defensive armament was a bit light at first for an American bomber with two .30in (7.62mm) Browning machine guns, one in the nose and the other in the tail. A Martin dorsal turret, the first power-operated turret to be fitted into an American-built bomber, with a pair of .50in (12.7mm) Browning machine guns, was positioned behind the bomb bay, forward of the tail. Bomb arrangements could vary with either a pair of 2,000lb carried internally or up to 4,800lb of smaller ordnance. In reality, the maximum bomb load would rarely exceed 4,000lb.

Eight early production B-26s on the ramp outside the Middle River factory, Baltimore on 5 March 1941. Three of the group have no propellers fitted at this stage because of a shortage of Curtiss electric propellers. (Via author)

'Foolproof' production

The Marauder was designed and built from the outset to be a mass-produced aircraft. Martin engineers confidently pre-empted a large order being received from the USAAF as the world situation continued to deteriorate. Martin also accurately predicted that the workforce required to build the bomber would have no, or very little, experience of building aircraft.

To help achieve the task of building a complex flying machine, the B-26 was put together from approximately 650 minor sub-assemblies, which were then joined to create 32 major sub-assemblies, and the final aircraft. All of the Marauder's frames and stringers were pre-drilled in their jigs and, once these components were delivered to the shop floor, the task of riveting was made all the easier.

The Marauder's fuselage was covered in 63 pieces of metal skin, each with its own compound curvature. Each piece of skin was produced on a stretch press with a high degree of accuracy and consistency that made the job of producing the B-26's streamlined fuselage quicker than bespoke panel beating.

Wing parts were also produced with the same degree of accuracy and consistency thanks to Martin working closely with a milling machine manufacturer to develop a machine with a travelling head and a 30ft bed. Every part of the wing was produced to be foolproof, basically meaning that the parts could only be fitted in one way – the correct one!

Salient differences

Because of the lack of a prototype and its swift entry into mass production, the B-26 would inevitably be developed on the run. This development saw the Marauder progress rapidly through eight different variants (A to G) and a production run which produced 5,268 aircraft between 1940 and April 1945.

B-26-MA (Baltimore-built)

The first production aircraft, B-26 40-1361 (c/n 1226), took to the air from Middle River, Baltimore on 25 November 1940 in the hands of chief engineer and test pilot, William K. 'Ken' Ebel. With no prototype, the vast majority of the first batch of 201 aircraft were either retained for development work or used for training. These bombers were simply referred to as the B-26. The first machine was not even designated with the prefix XB or YB as traditional, or with a suffix. Only minimal modifications were initiated on the first aircraft after 113 hours of flight testing and, on 22 February 1941, the first four B-26s were delivered to the USAAC. The customer was the 22nd BG (Medium) at Langley Field, Virginia, which was replacing its obsolete B-18s.

Early problems with front wheel strut failures may have been caused by a lack of communication between the manufacturer and the air force. A combination of the unusual tricycle arrangement and the high landing speed resulted in many failures during the 22nd BG's first few months with the B-26. The problem was attributed to the fact that Martin had to deliver the first B-26s without guns and, to trim them for delivery to Langley, service tools and spare parts were loaded as ballast. On arrival the ballast was removed but not replaced, which caused the centre of gravity to move forward, putting extra load onto the nose wheel. The problem was rectified once guns were added but, in the meantime, Martin strengthened the nose wheel strut before the exact problem was discovered.

At least a dozen forward fuselages of B-26-MAs from the initial order for 201 aircraft are visible in this production view in Martin's Middle River factory. The fuselage was built in three sections, not only to allow for easy transportation but also to aid repair.
(USAAF via author)

B-26	
Power	Two 1,850hp Pratt & Whitney R-2800-5 Double Wasp
Dimensions	Span, 65ft
	Length, 56ft
	Height, 19ft 10in
	Wing area, 602sq ft
	Wing loading, 53.2lb/sq ft
Weights	Empty, 21,375lb
	Normal take-off, 30,000lb
	Gross, 32,000lb
Performance	Max speed, 315mph at 15,000ft
	Cruising speed, 258mph
	Landing speed, 135mph
	Climb rate, 1,500ft/min
	Service ceiling, 25,000ft
	Range, 1,000 miles
Armament	Three .50in and two .30in machine guns, up to 5,200lb bomb load
Production	201; f/f 40-1361, 25 Nov, 1940
Serials	40-1361 to 40-1561

B-26A-MA, A-1-MA, Marauder I & IA

By October 1941, the last B-26 had been delivered and all focus was on producing the B-26A. It was only now that the bomber finally gained a proper name, which initially hovered around 'Martian' but was changed to 'Marauder'. From the outside, the B-26A appeared no different from its predecessor but several internal changes were applied. These included additional Dural armour, Goodyear self-sealing fuel tanks (which replaced the original Mareng-type tanks) and a set of mounts for a ferry tank in the rear bomb bay. The electrics

The cockpit of a B-26-MA photographed on 18 February 1941, only four days before the first aircraft were delivered to the US Army Air Corps. As with the majority of aircraft constructed during World War II, cockpits were subject to revision and redesigns of the layout. In the case of the Marauder, the cockpit was revised for the B-26B and C and the B-26F and G. (USAAF via author)

were beefed up from 12v to 24v and a 100amp generator was fitted. Shackles, which could be fitted on the outside of the bomb bay to enable the carriage of a 2,000lb 22in torpedo or a pair of 1,600lb bombs, were also made available. The .30in machine gun in the nose was replaced by a single .50in and the necessary pipework for a second jettisonable 250gal fuel tank in the forward bomb bay was another change. Finally, the B-26A-MA also introduced a new low-pressure oxygen system. This array of modifications inevitably made the B-26 heavier by 2,000lb.

The 'A-1' came about because of a shortage of R-2800-5 engines in the autumn of 1941, forcing the USAAF to order Pratt & Whitney to move 200 1,850hp R-2800-S1A-4G and 222 2,000hp R-2800-2SB-G engines from an RAF order. These engines were redesignated by the USAAF as R-2800-39s and R-2800-41s. The change in engine came from aircraft number 41-7366 and, other than the powerplant, the B-26A-1MA was the same as the B-26A-MA.

B-26A-MA	
Power	B-26A: Two 1,850hp Pratt & Whitney R-2800-5 Double Wasp
	B-26A-1: Two 1,850hp Pratt & Whitney R-2800-39 or 2,000hp -41 Double Wasp
Dimensions	Span, 65ft
	Length, 56ft
	Height, 19ft 10in
	Wing area, 602sq ft
	Wing loading, 53.2lb/sq ft
Weights	Empty, 23,375lb
	Normal take-off, 32,000lb
	Gross, 34,000lb
Performance	Max speed, 315mph at 15,000ft
	Cruising speed, 258mph
	Climb rate, 1,500ft/min
	Service ceiling, 25,000ft
	Range, 1,000 miles
Armament	Four .50in and one .30in machine guns, 4,800lb bomb load
Production	(B-26A) 30; (B-26A-1) 109
Serials	B-26A-MA & Marauder I: 41-7345 to 41-7365, 41-7368, 41-7431 & 41-7477 to 41-7483; FK109 to FK112, FK117, FK122 to FK124, FK133, FK134, FK137, FK142, FK143 & FK145, all to the RAF as Marauder Is
	B-16A-1 & Marauder I & IA: 41-7366 to 41-7367, 41-7369 to 41-7430 & 41-7432 to 41-7476; FK113 to FK116, FK118 to FK121, FK126 to FK132, FK135, FK136, FK138 to FK141, FK144 to FK146 and FK147 to FK160 all delivered to RAF as Marauder Is; FK362 to FK380 all delivered to RAF as Marauder IAs

B-26B-MA, B-1-MA, B-2MA & B-3MA

By April 1942, production of the B-26B had begun, although even this mark would be steadily improved as the 1,883 built were constructed in ten production batches. Initial modifications began with the first 100 aircraft built and the first of these were delivered to the USAAF on 5 April 1942; all were designated as the B-26B-MA. Modifications included additional armour and torpedo racks were by then fitted as standard. A further two .50in machine guns were later added in the lower waist position to give added protection from below. The tail gunner's position was also modified into a 'stepped' design and the rear fuselage was lengthened by 28in and fitted with a pair of .50in guns in place of the single .30in. The powerplants reverted from the R-2800-39 back to the original R-2800-5s and the oil cooler air intake under the cowling of each engine was increased in size.

From mid-1942, the majority of B-26Bs being built were destined to serve with units in North Africa but before they departed, 207 Marauders were diverted to Martin's Modification Centre in Omaha to be modified as the B-26B-1-MA. The latter was an official designation that was applied purely because of the large amount of modifications carried out.

The changes included strengthening the Plexiglas in the nose to take a single, flexibly mounted, .50in machine gun and a second .50in was placed in a fixed forward-firing position on the lower starboard side of the nose. The original .30in machine guns in the waist positions were replaced by a pair of .50in machine guns on flexible mounts, complemented by a pair of circular lenses above each gun to improve visibility for the gunner.

A B-26B Marauder of the 558th BS, 387th BG based at Chipping Ongar in Essex from June 1943 to July 1944. This particular aircraft is a B-50-MA, 42-95930 which was brought down by flak on 12 October 1944 after the 387th BG had relocated to Chateaudun/A-39 in France. (Via author)

Fuel capacity was increased to 1,962gal, giving the B-26B-1-MA a maximum ferry range of 2,850 miles and this was supported by the ability to carry another pair of 250gal ferry tanks in the rear bomb bay. The downside to this impressive increase in range was a rise in the take-off weight, which went up to 36,500lb. More power would obviously be needed and from the 306th aircraft off the production line, the engines were upgraded to the R-2800-41 or 43, both rated at 1,920hp apiece.

Specific modifications for desert operations included increasing the size of the air intakes on top of the engine cowling to accommodate the bigger dust filters and the original large propeller spinners were removed to help improve cooling, reduce weight and cut down on unnecessary maintenance. Finally, the B-26B-1-MA was fitted with slotted flaps to try and reduce the Marauder's high landing speed.

As Pratt & Whitney worked tirelessly to develop their R-2800 engine, the B-26 benefitted from every new upgraded powerplant. By May 1942, the engine manufacturer raised the horsepower of the R-2800-41 to 2,000hp, benefitting 95 Marauders that were designated as the B-26B-2-MA. The first of these was delivered to the USAAF on 17 June 1942.

The latest Marauder variant also incorporated one modification for a new VHF radio, which needed a whip-type aerial fitted on the under-fuselage, just behind the nose wheel door.

During the autumn of 1942, 28 B-26s were fitted with modified R-2800-43 engines, which were 'tweaked' to give a take-off rating of 2,000hp each. Only 28 aircraft were fitted with this powerplant, receiving the designation B-26B-3-MA. All of these aircraft had also received the same modifications as the B-26B-1.

B-26B-MA, B-1-MA, B-2-MA & B-3MA	
Power	B-26B & B-1: Two 1,850hp Pratt & Whitney R-2800-5 Double Wasp
	B-1 & B-3: Later two 1,920hp R-2800-41 or 43
	B-2: Two 2,000hp Pratt & Whitney R-2800-41 Double Wasp
Dimensions	Span, 71ft
	Length, 58ft 3in
	Height, 21ft 6in
	Wing area, 658sq ft
	Wing loading, 58.05lb/sq ft
Weights	Empty, 24,000lb
	Normal take-off, 37,000lb
Performance	Max speed, 282mph at 15,000ft
	Cruising speed, 260mph
	Climb rate, 1,500ft/min
	Service ceiling, 23,500ft
	Range, 1,150 miles
Fuel capacity	All B-26B and C models, 962gal (US)
Armament	Eight .50in machine guns and two .30in in waist, 3,000lb bomb load or a 2,000lb torpedo
Production	B: 100
	B-1: 207
	B-2: 95
	B-3: 28
Serials	B: 41-17544 to 41-17624 & 41-17626 to 41-17644
	B-1: 41-17645 to 41-17851
	B-2: 41-17852 to 41-17946
	B-4: 41-17625, 41-17947 to 41-17973

B-26B-4-MA

This variant came into production at Baltimore from September 1942 from the 431st aircraft. The weight was by now becoming critical and, thanks to even more equipment and increased armament, the wing loading rose to 63lb/sq ft. Those B-26B-4s destined for the North African theatre were fitted as per the B-26B-1, but the latest variant also included the following modifications.

Most significant was an attempt to improve the take-off performance of the B-26 by extending the nose undercarriage strut by 6in, effectively raising the angle of attack of the wing and giving the B-4 a noticeable nose-up attitude.

For the first time, the main undercarriage doors were closed mechanically. The doors were constructed in three parts, two of which were closed while the undercarriage was down, reducing the amount of drag. In the cockpit, both the pilot and co-pilot gained a retractable circular air ventilator, making the environment more comfortable in hot climates.

Armament was improved again with four .50in, two on each side of the forward fuselage in packages, giving the aircraft considerably more punch in the event of a head-on attack, and even the ability to strafe at low level.

B-26B-4-MA	
Power	Two 2,000hp Pratt & Whitney R-2800-43 Double Wasp
Production	200
Armament	Twelve .50in machine guns
Serials	41-17974 to 41-18184

How To Bail Out of the Marauder

LIFE VEST SHOULD BE WORN UNDER PARACHUTE
HARNESS ON ALL OVERWATER FLIGHTS

DINGHY   CHUTE

PILOT
CO-PILOT
NAVIGATOR
UPPER TURRET GUNNER
RADIO OPERATOR
TUNNEL GUNNER
TAIL GUNNER

All routes appear to lead to a rapid exit via the bomb bay in this official Martin-produced cutaway. It would definitely have been a tight squeeze through the opening in the two bomb bay bulkheads. (Via author)

B-26C-5-MO & C-6-MO (Omaha-built)

By January 1942, production capability was increased when Martin opened a new factory at Omaha, Nebraska. To distinguish Baltimore- and Omaha-built aircraft, the designation 'MO' was added to all Nebraska-built machines while the Block numbering continued to follow that which had already been set. However, even though the aircraft being built at Omaha were basically B-26Bs, to distinguish them further they were designated the B-26C. The first of them, the B-26C-5-MO, was rolled out in August 1942.

The C-5 introduced a host of modifications of its own, the most significant being the attempt by Martin to reduce the wing loading; they achieved this by increasing the span and chord, therefore increasing the area, which in turn reduced the loading to a more respectable 51.5lb/sq ft. There was always going to be a downside though and the aircraft's maximum speed fell to 282mph and the cruising speed to 214mph. The range also suffered, especially with a maximum fuel and bomb load.

The tail area was increased, which along with the length and the wing modifications saw the weight rise overall by 1,500lb. Other modifications included larger main wheels, which rose in diameter from 47 to 50in, and which needed an aerodynamic bulge to be moulded into the doors to take them.

The hydraulic system was improved, flame dampers were fitted to the engine exhausts and the generator was given a boost from the original 100amp type to a 200amp version. The back of the co-pilot's seat was shortened to improve access to the nose area of the B-26 and the armament arrangement of the B-26B-1 and B-4's gun packages became a standard fit.

The waist gun doors were improved by moving them one station rearwards and, by enlarging them, the field of fire was increased vertically and forward. A circular window was also added above the waist gun doors in place of the two smaller ones, which also improved visibility.

The racks and hoisting equipment in the bomb bay were modified for the better and the bombardier was given a better station to work in, with a section of optically flat glass, giving him a much better view during the bomb run. The nose and main undercarriage doors could close when extended to improve the aerodynamics from the 61st production aircraft.

The USAAF demanded that the B-26 should be reduced in weight in an effort to improve its take-off and landing performance. A batch of B-26C-5-MOs, all allocated to the 323rd BG, which was moving to England in 1943, were chosen to be lightened. This was achieved by removing the co-pilot's seat, his control column, some armour plating and several pieces of aircraft equipment.

Two squadrons of the 323rd BG flew the aircraft, designated the B-26C-6-MO, into combat, but senior commanders were far from happy about the lack of the co-pilot's position. The idea was quickly shelved and all 49 lightened B-26C-6-MOs were later converted back to their original crew configuration.

The Martin upper turret of a 322nd BG B-26 with its reflector sight removed to expose how the ammunition fed into the twin .50in Browning machine guns. The gunner is Sgt Stark. (USAAF via author)

B-26C-5-MO & C-6-MO	
Power	Two 2,000hp Pratt & Whitney R-2800-43 Double Wasp
Dimensions	Span, 71ft
	Length, 58ft 3in
	Height, 21ft 6in
	Wing area, 713sq ft
	Wing loading, 51.5lb/sq ft
Weights	Basic, 26,300lb
	Normal take-off, 31,200lb
	Loaded, 37,000lb
Performance	Max speed, 282mph at 15,000ft
	Cruising speed, 214mph
	Climb rate, 1,500ft/min
	Service ceiling, 23,500ft
	Range (962gal of fuel and 4,000lb bomb load), 550 miles
Armament	Twelve .50in machine guns, 4,000lb bomb load
Production	C-5: 175
	C-6: 49
Serials	C-5: 41-34673 to 41-34847
	C-6: 41-34681, 41-34689 to 41-34693, 41-34695, 41-34702 to 41-34742 & 41-34777 to 41-34787

B-26B-10-MA, B-15MA, C-10-MO & C-15-MO

Aircraft essentially the same as the B-26B-10 were built at Omaha, and later designated the B-26C. The new variant differed little from the previous one, being built with the same longer span wing, bigger fin and rudder. As with the B-models before it, the longer wing and larger fin did nothing for the aircraft's performance as by then the maximum speed had decreased to 282mph and the cruising speed to a woeful 214mph.

This B-15 variant only differed from its predecessor, the B-10, by having the Type A-9 oxygen regulator taken out and the new SCR (Signal Corps Radio) -595A IFF (Identification Friend or Foe) equipment fitted. The 100 Baltimore-built aircraft were serialled 41-31573 to 41-31672. These same changes were also applied at Omaha, resulting in the C-15, serialled 41-34908 to 41-34997.

B-26B-10-MA, B-15-MA, B-26C-10-MO & C-15-MO	
Power	(all variants) Two 2,000hp Pratt & Whitney R-2800-43 Double Wasp
Dimensions	Span, 71ft
	Length, 58ft 3in
	Height, 21ft 6in
	Wing area, 658sq ft
	Wing loading, 58.05lb/sq ft
Weights	Empty, 24,000lb
	Normal take-off, 37,000lb
Performance	Max speed, 282mph at 15,000ft
	Cruising speed, 214mph
	Climb rate, 1,500ft/min
	Service ceiling, 23,500ft
	Range, 1,150 miles
Armament	Twelve .50in machine guns, 3,000lb bomb load
Production	(B-10) 150; (B-15) 100; (C-10) 60; (C-15) 90
Serials	(B-10) 41-18185 to 41-18334; (B-15) 41-31573 to 41-31672; (C-10) 41-34848 to 41-34907; (C-15) 41-34908 to 41-34997

B-26B-20-MA, B-25-MA, C-20-MO & C-25-MO

The B-20/C-20 variant introduced a new power-operated electromechanical Bell M-6 turret in place of the twin hand-held .50in machine guns in the tail position. The M-6 turret changed the shape of the rear fuselage to such an extent that the overall length was reduced to 56ft 1in. The only other difference was a new short chord rudder.

Modifications to the armament and crew protection resulted in the B-25/C-25, of which 398 were built. Extra armour plating was fitted around the Martin 250CE turret. Additionally, on the C-25 a collection pan was placed below the tail guns to collect empty cartridge cases.

B-26B-20-MA, B-25-MA, B-26C-20-MO & C-25-MO	
Production	B-20: 100
	B-25: 100
	C-20: 175
	C-25: 298
Serials	B-20: 41-31673 to 41-31772
	B-25: 41-31773 to 41-31872
	C-20: 41-34998 to 41-35172
	C-25: 41-35073 to 41-35370

The sting in the tail of the B-26 was the Bell M-6 turret fitted with a pair of .50in machine guns. This view of a ground crewman servicing the turret shows how the Plexiglas canopy is raised to expose the flexible feed track for the ammunition and the thick armour plate in front of the gunner, which could stop a 20mm round. (USAAF via author)

B-26B-30-MA, B-35-MA, B-40MA, C-30-MO, C-35-MO, C-40MO & Marauder II

As with the previous variant, the only changes centred around fitting further protection for the crew. First, a single piece of curved armour plate was placed on the port side of the fuselage to help protect the pilot. Secondly, another piece of armour plate was placed behind the bomb-aimer's position as well as several important systems throughout the aircraft.

The Omaha-built B-26C-30s were delivered to the RAF as FB415 to FB517 and redesignated the Marauder II. The only modification to the B-35/C-35 variant was the removal of the alcohol de-icing system for the engine's carburettors. The B-40/C-40 variant incorporated a few subtle changes, which included the addition of a torpedo-firing switch on the pilot's control column and the discontinuation of the Type B-2 Torpedo Director. From 42-43310 onwards, 'shark nose' ailerons were also introduced.

B-26B-30-MA, B-35-MA, B-40-MA & B-26C-30-MO, C-35-MO & C-40-MO	
Production	B-30: 100
	B-35: 100
	B-40: 200
	C-30: 200
	C-35: 200
	C-40: 100
Serials	B-30: 41-31873 to 41-31972
	B-35: 41-31973 to 41-32072
	B-40: 42-43260 to 42-43459, 42-43360, 4243361 & 42-43459
	C-30: 41-35373 to 41-35572;
	FB415 to FB517 delivered to RAF as Marauder II
	C-35: 41-35572 to 41-35772
	C-40: 41-35773 to 41-35872

B-26B-45-MA, B-50-MA, B-55-MA & C-45-MO

Block 45 of the continuing B-26B and C range saw another string of subtle modifications, some of which, by this stage of the war, were being incorporated as a result of combat experience.

To help the pilot to aim the four package guns either side of the forward fuselage, he was equipped with a gun sight mounted on top of his panel. Other armament-related modifications included fitting stronger bomb hooks and, following the USAAF's decision to remove the requirement to carry 100lb bombs, the rear bomb bay was bolted shut. It was instead used for the storage of .50in ammunition for the rear gunner and which transited to the tail via a 28ft track. Further armament changes saw the single fixed .50in machine gun in the nose deleted from 42-95979.

Aircraft equipment was improved with a new SCR-695 IFF system and a SCR-522 VHF command radio set plus a new remote heading compass. Finally, the Block 45 aircraft had the engine fire extinguisher refitted.

Block 50 B-26Bs were built at the Baltimore plant. This variant was fitted with a mechanical mechanism for closing the bomb bay doors in the event of an emergency. An updated and modified IFF system was also installed and, from 42-95942 onwards, the B-26B-50-MA was fitted with Lycoming propeller blades.

Block 55 B-26Bs were also all built at Baltimore and represented the last batch of the most prolifically produced model of the Marauder range. This block saw the standard D-8 bombsight replaced by the Carl L. Norden M-series sight and, from 42-96079 onwards, various modifications were made to the Martin 250CE turret including a new optical sight. From 42-96129 all B-26s built at Baltimore left the plant devoid of a camouflaged finish.

B-26B-45-MA, B-50-MA, B-55-MA & B-26C-45-MO		
Production	B-45: 200	
	B-50: 200	
	B-55: 200	
	C-45: 359	
Serials	B-45: 42-95629 to 42-95828	
	B-50: 42-95829 to 42-96028	
	B55: 42-96029 to 42-96228	
	C-45: 42-107497 to 42-107855	

XB-26D

Quite a few early B-26s found themselves being utilized for specialist tasks, although very few of them were given any kind of designation to give away this fact. However, one aircraft that did was B-26 40-1380 which, after service with 22nd BG, was modified into the one and only XB-26D. The main use for the bomber was to test a de-icing system, which diverted hot air from the engines via a heat exchanger and fed the air to the leading edges of the wings and tail surfaces. Despite the modification being a success, the USAAF deemed that the system would disrupt production too much and the idea was shelved.

C **B-26C MARAUDER**
B-26C-45-MO, 42-107811 'IH-H' of the 1st Pathfinder Squadron (Provisional) based at Andrews Field, Essex, as flown by Lt Edward B. Fitch. The aircraft was later transferred to the 575th BS, 391st BG based at Matching (also in Essex), only to be lost over Normandy on 5 July 1944.

A rare image of the sole XB-26E, ex-B-26C 41-34680, which was named *Gypsy Rose* after a well-known strip-tease dancer named Gypsy Rose Lee. The aircraft was extensively modified, including the relocation of the Martin dorsal turret in the radio operator's compartment. (USAAF via author)

XB-26D	
Technical date	*as per B-26*
Production	1
Serial	40-1380

XB-26E & B-26E

The designation XB-26E was an unofficial one that was applied to one aircraft, namely B-26C 41-34680, later nicknamed *Gypsy Rose*. The object of the exercise was to produce a significantly lighter B-26, and a single B-26C was taken from the Omaha production line in January 1943. The bomber was stripped of all unnecessary equipment including the navigator's seat; only basic navigational equipment was left in place. Surplus radio equipment was removed, as was the entire oxygen system, electrically heated clothing connectors and outlets, the rear bomb bay racks and even the toilet.

Gypsy Rose was now 2,600lb lighter than a standard B-26C, which would have made the bomber a spritely performer. Further modifications to the bomber saw the Martin dorsal turret moved forward to a position above the radio operator's compartment. This instantly improved the field of fire and unexpectedly improved the aircraft's handling in the air as well. Once again, though, the cost and disruption that would be caused to the established production lines saw the advantages achieved by the XB-26E outweighed.

By March 1943, *Gypsy Rose* was delivered to Wright Field for further flight testing and, following recommendations by test pilots, several modifications were subtly introduced into the production line. There would undoubtedly have been recommendations for the removal of certain surplus equipment, which would have done nothing to harm the speed of production.

Two other versions of the Marauder were also unofficially referred to as the B-26E; the first of these was a ground-attack strafing variant while the second was a modified bomber. One aircraft, B-26B 42-43319 was used for the ground-attack variant and was extensively armed with a pair of 37mm cannon and two .50in machine guns in a modified nose, and the four .50in machine guns in packages either side of the forward fuselage. Additional windows were also fitted behind the new nose to help improve visibility downwards and additional armour was fitted around all of the crew stations. Trials were also carried out with a double-tube rocket launcher under the forward fuselage. The concept worked well and modifications barely disrupted the aircraft's handling but, by this time, the role the B-26 was attempting to break into was already being successfully carried out by the P-47 Thunderbolt.

The bomber B-26E[1] was another ex-B-26B Marauder which made use of the same forward turret position of the XB-26E. This aircraft was nothing more than a limited development version of the XB-26E, attempting to continue the idea of a lightweight bomber version with better-positioned armament but, once again, it was destined never to enter production.

XB-26E & B-26E	
Technical data	As per B-26C
Weights	Empty, 21,400lb
	Normal take-off, 34,400lb
Performance	Max speed, well over 300mph
Armament	XB-26E: twelve .50in machine guns
	B-26E 'Ground-Attack': two 37mm cannon and two .50in machine guns in modified, plus eight .50in machine guns in standard positions
Production	3
Serials	XB-26E: 41-34680
	B-26E 'Ground-Attack': 42-43319
	B-26E 'Bomber': unknown

B-26F-1-MA, F-2-MA, F-6-MA & Marauder III

The penultimate main production variant of the Marauder first emerged from the Baltimore factory (all B-26Fs would be built at Baltimore) in February 1944. The B-26F was another attempt to improve the flying characteristics of the Marauder by changing the incidence of the wing by a further 3.5 degrees to 7 degrees. This relatively small adjustment increased the ground clearance for the propellers, reduced the take-off run, lowered the landing speed and gave the bomber more lift. In the air the B-26F flew in a more level attitude, rather than the slightly nose-high position of the previous variants. There was always a downside though: the maximum speed dropped to 277mph and the bomber's handling characteristics were not as crisp as earlier models.

Armament modifications saw the removal of the long-redundant torpedo shackles and an electric bomb release system helped to reduce any hang-ups in the bay. The single fixed .50in in the nose was also removed and the bomb load was increased back up to the original 4,000lb.

Other internal changes saw the fitment of an improved fuel transfer system and a cross-feed for the main tanks, which were increased in size to cater for 2,500gal (US) of fuel. A new oil cooler and thermostatic control and surge valve was fitted from 42-96231 and the trailing antenna became detachable. The instrument panel was given a facelift and the B-26F was fitted with new lower wing access panels to make life easier for the groundcrew.

1 Official documents have suggested that the 'E' suffix was to be applied to the B-26B-1, which had been modified with an increased 3 degree positive camber wing for improved performance. An increased 3.5 degrees was later introduced into the production line for the B-26F and B-26G and 'E', which was to be applied to the 'twisted wing' variants, was discarded by November 1943.

The final, and one of the most significant modifications introduced by this variant, was a new emergency landing gear system. In normal circumstances, the B-26's undercarriage was lowered hydraulically, but very often, if the system was damaged or failed, the wheels would lock up. The only option available to the crew was gravity at this stage and if that did not work, it was time to take to the chute or prepare for a belly landing. The new system allowed the undercarriage to be mechanically released and if it was not damaged, the wheels would simply drop into the airflow and lock into place. Several B-26Fs and the final B-26Gs were fitted with a tail bumper to protect the lower rear fuselage during take-off and landing.

All 200 of the B-26F-2s and F-6s were built for the RAF and South African Air Force (SAAF) and, in service, were designated as the Marauder III. The aircraft had several subtle differences from their USAAF counterparts including the replacement of the Bell M-6 tail turret with an M-6A, which differed by having a canvas cover around the end of the gunner's position. All flexibly mounted machine guns were fitted with optical sights and the Sperry Gyroscope T-1 bombsight was replaced by the M-series. Other armament-related modifications included fitting B-9 bomb shackles and provision was made for British nose and tail bomb fusing. The bomber's radio equipment was the final adjustment, which saw them modified to RAF and SAAF standards.

Bespoke trailers were used for delivering bombs to the B-26; from these the 500lb M43 bombs were placed into jacking frames which were lifted into the bay. The aircraft here is B-26B-25-MA, 41-31847, *Jolly Roger* of the 322nd BG. (USAAF via author)

B-26F-1-MA, F-2-MA, F-6-MA & Marauder III	
Technical data	*As per B-26B/C*
Power	Two Pratt & Whitney R-2800-43 engines
Performance	Max speed, 277mph
Fuel capacity	All B-26F and G models, 1,002gal (US)
Armament	Eleven .50in machine guns; Bomb load, 4,000lb
Production	F-1: 100
	F-2: 200
Serials	F-1: 42-96229 to 42-96328
	F-2: 42-96329 to 42-96428, to RAF as HD402 to HD501
	F-6: 42-96429 to 42-96528, to RAF as HD502 to HD601

 D

1: MARAUDER IA (14 SQUADRON)
Ex 41-7429 B-26A-1 redesignated as a Marauder IA in RAF service and re-seriallied FK370. This aircraft was the lead aircraft, flown by Maj Lewis SAAF on the Melos harbour raid on 21 February 1943.

2: B-26G-5-MA (444TH BS, 320TH BG)
Pancho and his Reever Rats, a B-26G-5-MA, serialed 43-34240, served with the 444th BS, 320th BG from Decimomannu in Sardinia. On 23 August 1944, whilst attacking a roadblock at Covigliaio, the Marauder took a direct hit and exploded, killing all seven crew on board.

3: B-26G-25-MA (GBM 1/34)
The last of six Groupe de Bombardement (GBM) to be equipped with the B-26 was I/32 'Bourgogne' based at St Dizier. The Groupe flew the B-26G-25-MA from September 1944 until June 1945.

4: JM-1 (EX AT-23B) (USMC)
There were 225 JM-1s supplied to the US Navy and US Marine Corps, including 66758 'U8', which is depicted as it would have appeared in January 1945.

1

2

3

4

B-26G-1-MA, G-5-MA, G-10-MA, Marauder III & G-11-MA

The final production mark of the Marauder began to roll out of the Baltimore factory in March 1944 and, like the B-26F before, all would be built at the Middle River plant. The B-26G was no different from the B-26F on the outside but internal equipment differed in several areas.

The B-26G-1 changes began with a new C-1 autopilot fitted from aircraft 43-34190 as requested by the Ninth Air Force. All internal equipment was brought up to a new 'Universal Army & Navy' standard and both the inboard and outboard fuel tanks in the wings were connected by a cross-feed system. The life raft compartment in the upper fuselage was made bigger so that it could hold a bigger A-3 or E-2 dinghy complete with survival provisions and radio. The forward fuselage on earlier variants had been suffering from the effects of blast from the four fuselage-mounted package guns and, to protect the structure, a section of armour was added.

The B-26G-5-MA only differed from the G-1 in having a slightly

This photo entitled 'Bomb Bay Door Open' gives an excellent view of how the B-26 utilized the forward bay only while the rear was sealed, being used for an extra fuel tank instead. The aircraft are from the 320th BG, captured during an attack on the Incisa railway bridge, south of Florence in April 1944. (Via author)

modified hydraulic system. The G-10 and G-11 aircraft both introduced a few more subtle changes to the breed. Under the tail gunner's position, a cartridge case collector was fitted as standard and the cowl flap lock valve system was discarded from aircraft 43-34575 onwards. The only other change was the introduction of Lycoming propellers; several of these aircraft were fitted with them.

A total of 75 B-26G-10-MAs were diverted to the RAF as Marauder IIIs, serialled HD602 to HD676 (43-4465 to 43-4539). The vast majority of these Marauders were delivered to the Middle East but never joined an operational squadron.

B-26G-1-MA, G-5-MA, G-10-MA, Marauder III & G-11-MA	
Technical data	*As per B-26F*
Production	G-1: 100
	G-5: 200
	G-10 inc III: 125
	G-11: 75
Serials	G-1: 43-34115 to 43-34214
	G-5: 43-34215 to 43-34414
	G-10: 43-34415 to 43-34539 (HD602 to HD676 (75))
	G-11: 43-34540 to 43-34614

B-26G-15-MA, G-20-MA, G-21-MA Marauder III, TB-26G-15-MA & G-20-MA

The B-26G-15-MA only differed from its predecessor in having the C-1 autopilot removed and a new modified radio compass fitted. The last ten aircraft from this production run, which was completed in November 1944, were built as the TB-26G. These aircraft had all armament and combat equipment stripped out and were converted into target tugs or used for general training duties – a total of 57 were eventually modified for this new role. The ten TB-26Gs were later transferred to the US Navy and redesignated as the JM-2 (90507 to 90516).

The only minor modification on the G-20 and G-21 Marauders was whip-type static dischargers. In all, 15 Marauders of this batch were built as TB-26Gs, 75 were delivered to the RAF as Marauder IIIs and the remaining 60 were turned over to the USAAF. Of the TB-26Gs, 44-67955 to 44-67959 were transferred to the US Navy and redesignated JM-2s 90517 to 90521 while the remainder were retained by the USAAF.

Two becomes one was the result of *Half and Half* of the 322nd BG, which used the forward fuselage of *Goatee Hell* and the rear fuselage of *Weary Willie*. By the war's end, the rear fuselage had completed 160 missions and the front 134! (USAAF via author)

B-26G-15-MA, G-20-MA & G-21-MA, TB-26G-15-MA & G-20	
Technical data	As per B-26F
Production	G-15: 150
	G-20: 150
Serials	B: 44-67805 to 44-67944
	TB: 44-67945 to 44-67954
	G-20: 44-67970 to 44-67989 & 44-68065 to 44-68104
	G-21: 44-67990 to 44-68064 (HD677 to HD751)
	TB: 44-67955 to 44-67969

B-26G-25-MA & TB-26G-25-MA

The last production variant of a long line of B-26 Marauders, along with all those before it, introduced a few subtle modifications. A total of 32 of this final production were built as TB-26Gs, the work to convert them being carried out in March 1945. All of them went on to serve with the US Navy as JM-2s with the serials 91962 to 91993.

The last new-build Martin B-26 Marauder, B-26G-25-MA 44-68254 named *Tail End Charlie*, was delivered from Baltimore on 18 April 1945.

B-26G-25-MA & TB-26G-25-MA	
Technical data	*As per B-26F*
Production	150
Serials	B: 44-68105 to 44-68221 & 44-68254
	TB: 44-68222 to 44-68253

CB-26B

Twelve B-26Bs were modified into transport aircraft, all of them being delivered to the United States Marine Corps (USMC) for operations around the Philippines. The prototype CB-26B is believed to have been the second production B-26B 41-17545. The aircraft was fitted with a solid nose, all armament was removed and late-model engine carburettor air intakes were added.

AT-23A (TB-26B) & AT-23B (TB-26C)

Another conversion of the B-26 that saw service in large numbers during World War II was the AT-23, later redesignated the TB-26. The aircraft filled a valuable gap in the training of air gunners at high altitudes, an area that, up to 1943, had no aircraft capable of fulfilling the role. The requirement for a high-flying target-towing aircraft actually came from operational combat units who were worried that their air gunners were not achieving the level of success that had been hoped for. All training up to this period was carried out at much lower levels, where the air is thicker and a bullet must overcome greater air resistance. In combat at higher altitudes in thinner air, bullets' trajectories were different to those that gunners had experienced in training.

By 1943 Marauders were steadily becoming more readily available, making the aircraft the prime candidate for conversion as a target tug and general utility aircraft. The first aircraft to be converted were a batch of 208 B-26Bs, which were redesignated AT-23A. All armour and armament was removed and the dorsal turret blanked off. A C-5 target-towing winch, complete with target carriers, was installed in their place.

Such was the demand that a further 300 B-26Cs were converted in the same way but redesignated AT-23B. By 1944, the two variants were redesignated as TB-26B and the TB-26C.

AT-23 & TB-26	
Technical data	As per B-26B & B-26C
Production	AT-23A/TB-26B: 208
	AT-23B/TB-26C: 350
Serials	AT-23A/TB-26B: 42-43358, 42-43359, 42-43362 to 42-43458 & 42-95629 to 42-95737
	AT-23B/TB-26C: 41-35071, 41-35370 to 41-35373, 41-35525 to 41-35572, 41-35598 to 41-35620, 41-35773 to 41-35872, 42-107471 to 42-107496 & 42-107831 to 42-107855

JM-1, JM-1P & JM-2

The US Navy and USMC also had need for high-altitude target towers for gunnery training. In naval hands, the aircraft were redesignated as JM-1 (ex-AT-23B/TB-26C) and the JM-2 (ex-TB-26G). The aircraft were operated in the same way and with the same equipment as per their USAAF days, but in contrast to their previous unpainted appearance, the Navy machines were usually painted bright yellow all over. A few JM-1s were modified to JM-1P standard, indicating a dedicated photographic use.

JM-1 & JM-2	
Technical data	*As per B-26B & B-26C*
Production	JM-1: 225
	JM-2: 47
Serials	JM-1: 66595 to 66794 & 75183 to 75207
	JM-2: 90522 to 90531 & 91962 to 91993

Over 200 B-26s were converted into target tug/ trainers; all were from the B model and were originally designated as AT-23A and later TB-23B. The US Navy and US Marine Corps also flew the type as the JM-1, which is seen here flying over Greenland. (Via author)

39

OPERATIONAL HISTORY

Cutting its teeth in the Pacific

Thrown in at the deep end, the first operations flown by the B-26 were against the might of the Imperial Japanese Navy, which saw the USAAF's first and last use of the type in the torpedo-bomber role.

Rabaul and Lae Island

Following the attack on Pearl Harbor on 7 December 1941, the 22nd BG was transferred to Australia. The B-26s were disassembled and loaded onto ships at San Francisco before setting sail for Hawaii on 6 February 1942. On their arrival, the aircraft were unloaded and reassembled at Hickam Field. From there, the B-26s flew several coastal patrols before long-range ferry tanks were fitted into the bomb bays. The aircraft then set out for Australia, where the first aircraft landed at Brisbane on 22 March before transferring to Amberley Field under the command of Lt Gen H. Brett. The lengthy flight did not go without a hitch. At least one aircraft was lost without trace en route.

Not long after, the 22nd BG moved north to Townsville and it was from here, via Port Moresby, that the B-26 saw its first action against the Japanese base at Rabaul on 5 April, 1942. Only one bomber was lost on the first raid in a series of actions, which, despite heavy enemy opposition, proved to be very effective. The routine was to take off from mainland Australia with a 2,000lb bomb load (four 500lb or 20 100lb bombs) in one bomb bay and a 250gal fuel tank in the other. After refuelling at Port Moresby, the B-26s, which would operate in small formations ranging from two to no more than six aircraft, carried out a medium bombing raid at between 10,000ft and 15,000ft.

The B-26s of the 22nd and 38th BG quickly gained a good reputation for their performance and ability to stand up to a lot of punishment. Having no fighter escort of their own, the B-26 often managed to fend off and claim a few A6M Zeros shot down as well. After 80 operations, the attacks on Rabaul came to an end on 24 May 1942, by which time attention was being transferred to other targets throughout the East Indies. Japanese installations in the Lae and Salamaua Island area were next on the agenda and another 84 operations were flown between 24 April and 4 July 1942. Only three B-26s were lost during this period and the crews of the two bomb groups were full of praise for their aircraft.

Flak Bait, B-26B 41-31773, belonging to the 449th BS, 322nd BG, was one of a handful of aircraft that remained on the ground at Bury St Edmunds on 17 May 1942, when 12 bombers failed to return from the IJmuiden raid. Who would have thought, during this period of doubt for the B-26's very existence, that *Flak Bait* would become the only USAAF bomber to complete 200 operations, going on to achieve 207 before retirement? (Via author)

Midway and the Aleutians

Back at Hickam Field, a small group of B-26s from the 22nd and 38th BG had been left behind. Not only had the B-26B made its debut with the 38th BG, but also its capability as a torpedo bomber was about to be tested. The under-slung torpedo only cleared the ground by 4in, so operations could only take place from the smoothest of runways and great care had to be taken while taxying. The 39th BG began arriving in Hawaii from May 1942 onwards and, unlike their predecessors, the unit flew the 2,400 miles across the Pacific. During the final days of May, the 69th BS (Bombardment Squadron), 38th BG was chosen to practice the art of dropping torpedoes with just four crews, two of which were from the 22nd BG.

Led by Capt J. F. Collins Jr and 2nd Lt W. S. Watson from the 69th BS, with Lt J. P. Muri and Lt Herbert C. Mayes from the 18th RS(M), 22nd BG, the small force moved to Midway on 2 June 1942. It was here that the B-26s were prepared for the daunting task of attacking the approaching Japanese fleet. It was during the early hours of 4 June that orders came through for Capt Collins to prepare his small force. At 0630hrs, the B-26s headed west towards the Japanese fleet, which was spotted just 35 minutes later. Their priority targets were the enemy carriers, and they formed up with Collins in the lead, Watson and Mayes either side of him and Muri in *Suzie-Q* tucked in behind. But as the four-ship element descended to low level, six Zeros attacked the B-26s head-on. A woeful lack of nose armament saw no reply to the fighter attack and by now the bombers were just 200ft above the waves. Collins had selected the *Akagi* as his target and, with 800yd to run, he dropped his 2,000lb torpedo, closely followed by his three wingmen. All of the B-26s then began a series of evasive maneuvers in an attempt to avoid the relentless flak which seemed to be coming from all directions. Unfortunately, the *Akagi* had time enough to perform its own evasive manoeuvre and none of the torpedoes found their mark.

As the enemy began to retreat into their home territory, the 17th BG was moved to Dijon from where it attacked targets deep in Germany. These 95th BS Marauders have just attacked a V2 storage site at Siegelsbach in early 1945. The 17th BG, nicknamed 'The Daddy of Them All', went on to achieve 606 operational missions, the highest of any B-26 BG. (Via author)

In an moment of either madness or sheer brilliance, Lt Muri steered *Suzie-Q* directly down the line of the *Akagi's* flight deck, Muri's theory being that this was the only place that they stood a chance of not being shot at! Strafing as they went, the carrier fleet commander, Vice Adm C. Nagumo, who was on the bridge of *Akagi*, was forced to take cover along with many other crew, who must have been flabbergasted by the American flyer's cheek. As Muri was climbing away, he noticed another B-26 just missing the *Akagi's* superstructure before crashing into the sea. Which aircraft this was is unclear, but neither Lt Watson nor Lt Mayes nor their crews survived the daring operation.

Capt Collins and Lt Muri were very lucky to make it back to Midway, both having to crash-land due to damaged undercarriages. Collins' aircraft had gained over 180 holes from small arms and flak while *Suzie-Q* went one better with 500 holes, including all eight propeller blades damaged and all three air gunners wounded. Neither aircraft would fly again and after any useful equipment was stripped from them, they were dumped in the Pacific.

The same day, the Japanese also struck at the Aleutian Islands in the North Pacific with a force that included the carrier *Ryujo*. Unbeknown to the Japanese, the Americans had two airfields on the islands supporting the 28th BG, which was part of the Eleventh Air Force. Within the composite group was the 73rd BS, which was equipped with six B-26s. This was another chance for the aircraft to prove itself as a torpedo bomber and, after the enemy force was discovered by a Catalina, a pair of bombers took off from Randall Army Field, Cold Bay, in search of the *Ryujo*. Flown by Capt G. W. Thornbrough and H. S. Taylor, after entering a fog bank the two B-26s almost crashed into the carrier, before both dropping to sea level to carry out their torpedo attacks. Diving down to almost 350mph, Thornbrough released his torpedo only to see it land on the deck of the heaving carrier and then roll off harmlessly into the sea. Taylor carried out a similar attack and nearly hit the superstructure of the *Ryujo* in the process. Not long after, the B-26 was hit by flak followed by an attack from at least two Zeros, although one of these was claimed as shot down. Luckily for Taylor and his crew, the B-26 was sturdy enough to make the 100-mile flight back to Cold Bay. Thornbrough raced back to Randall Field undamaged, landed, refuelled, re-armed and set off again to have another go at the enemy carrier. Unfortunately, no trace of his B-26 was ever seen again. In his honour, Randall Field was renamed Thornbrough Field in 1948.

This was the last time that the B-26 was used as a torpedo bomber by the USAAF, after it was realized that the aircraft was simply too big for such a role. However, this would not stop the RAF using the Marauder briefly in the torpedo role in the Mediterranean and, comparatively speaking, achieving some successes. By early 1943, the B-26 was withdrawn from the Alaskan theatre to be replaced by the B-25.

Foreign service

Initially welcomed with open arms by the RAF, the Marauder was unfairly treated with suspicion and only went on to serve with two operational squadrons. It was the South African Air Force that used the type the most of the foreign air forces, followed to a lesser extent by the Free French Air Force.

14 Squadron RAF

The Marauder first entered service with 14 Squadron at Fayid, Egypt in August 1942. The unit had previously operated the obsolete Bristol Blenheim, albeit successfully, and was selected for re-equipment with the Marauder by the Commander in Chief (C-in-C) Middle East, Sir Arthur Tedder, later Lord Tedder. Thanks to Lend-Lease, the RAF and SAAF received 520 Marauders of various marks. The first batch of 52 Marauder Is was delivered between September and November 1942. The Mk I was the same as a B-26A, fitted with the original 65ft-span wings, and it was not long before the RAF was experiencing the same problems that had befallen the USAAF with the new type. Following trials by the A&AEE at Boscombe Down, which returned a very unfavourable report, many early Marauders were stockpiled with 161 MU at Fayid. The few Marauders that did become operational only served with 14 Squadron, and its aircraft included a second smaller batch of 19 Mk IAs. Of this batch, which was based on the B-26B, only two survived, to be struck off charge before the end of 1944.

14 Squadron began receiving the Marauder from 10 August 1942, the first of which arrived at LG 224 near Cairo. Aircrews found the bomber easy to handle and, thanks to a high level of maintenance by the ground crews, the accident rate was kept very low. So low that, during one three-month period in 1943, the squadron achieved the best flight safety record of the Mediterranean Allied Coastal Air Forces, recording a rate of one accident per 1,560 flying hours.

In August 1942, the squadron moved to Fayid from where the intensive conversion training continued, aided by virtually uninterrupted clear conditions. On 28 October 1942 14 Squadron flew its first operation; FK121 'Y', flown by the officer commanding (OC), Wg Cdr Dick Maydwell, flew a reconnaissance sortie over the Mediterranean. Over the next two months, the squadron focussed on flying anti-shipping sweeps, laying mines in Tunis harbour, and bombing raids on the airfield and railway facilities at Gabes in

Tunisia. All of these raids were moderately successful and, thanks to the arrival of B-26B, the unit also carried out several attacks using torpedoes, with mixed results. By December 1942, the latter became 14 Squadron's primary role and, from January 1943 onwards, they had mastered the technique and ships were being sunk. The first of these was a 1,500-ton ship which was successfully torpedoed by Fg Off Elliot in the Aegean Sea.

Wg Cdr Maydwell led a daylight operation on 10 January to lay mines in the Burgi Channel, north of Athens. Taking off from Shallufa, the three Marauders involved completed the operation in 8½ hours; a flight of 1,650 miles, all of which was flown at no more than 100ft! All three aircraft escaped detection and interception by enemy aircraft, partly because the operations were planned for midday, when it was hoped that the Italian gunners would be having a siesta; luckily this was the case. To drop their mines the Marauders had to

A 14 Squadron trio, led by Wg Cdr Dick Maydwell's aircraft, *Dominion Revenge* (FK375). The squadron operated the Marauder I, II and III between August 1942 and September 1944. FK375 was a short-span IA and was lost during an attack on a convoy off Agios Georgios Island on 3 January 1943. (Via author)

be flown at 50ft above the sea and as slow as possible, so if alert Germans had been manning the anti-aircraft guns, the outcome would have been very different. The magnetic mines were dropped in the narrow channel at Khalkis, the intention being to keep enemy ships out at sea where Royal Navy submarines were better able to attack them. Maydwell flew a similar operation on 14 February to the Burgi Channel, and information later received reported that at least one ship had been sunk by the mines and another had been damaged.

Another particularly successful raid using torpedoes took place on 21 February when Maj E. Lewis SAAF led nine Marauders against shipping in Melos harbour. One ship was sunk and another was damaged for the loss of two Marauders but, despite this success, this would be the last time the RAF used the type in the torpedo role.

By now, the longer-span Marauder II and III, based on the B-26F and B-26G respectively, had begun to arrive. Regardless, 14 Squadron remained the only RAF operational unit to fly the Marauder at that time and, following a move to Tunisia in March 1943, began serving with the North African Coastal Air Force. The squadron was now employed on anti-submarine operations, achieving a great deal of success with detachments from Corsica, Sardinia, Sicily and Italy. Flying in support of the Allied forces, by March 1944 the squadron had dropped 18,000 tons on tactical and strategic targets, which was no mean feat for a single medium-bomber unit.

Other victories achieved by 14 Squadron included the discovery of the Italian liner *Rex* in September 1944 and several Messerschmitt Me 323s claimed as shot down during its tour in the Mediterranean. One of the latter encounters occurred whilst the unit was operating out of Bone when a large formation of German and Italian Air Force transport aircraft was intercepted. By the end of the engagement, Wg Cdr Maydwell had shot down an Me 323,

a Savoia-Marchetti SM.82 and probably destroyed a Junkers Ju 90. Sqn Ldr Donovan even claimed a Messerschmitt Bf 109 shot down and other pilots from 14 Squadron also brought down another SM.82 and a pair of Ju 52/3ms. The Marauder period came to an end in October when 14 Squadron was transferred to Chivenor to convert to Wellingtons, leaving the RAF temporarily without an operational Marauder squadron. During 14 Squadron's 26 months of Marauder operations, the unit had lost 39 aircraft – 22 of these to enemy action and 17 to accidents.

39 Squadron RAF

With the RAF now awash with later Marauder IIIs, one final unit was re-equipped with the type, namely 39 Squadron, in late December 1944 under the command of Wg Cdr De Inniss. Operating from Biferno, the unit saw out the remainder of the war flying bombing operations against targets in Yugoslavia as part of the Balkan Air Force in support of the partisans led by Marshal Tito.

The first operation was flown on 7 February 1945 when 12 Marauders attacked the railway station and marshalling yards at Senje. Three boxes of four aircraft apiece bombed from 6,500ft, scoring a few hits in the target area, which were later confirmed from bombing photographs.

39 Squadron went on to fly 63 operations against targets in Yugoslavia, all without the loss of an aircraft, although many returned with such extensive flak damage that they were struck off charge. With a complete lack of enemy opposition in the air and flak becoming less frequent, April 1945 saw 39 Squadron flying every single day, sometimes twice daily throughout the month. Between 3 April and 13 April, double operations were flown most days. On average, 24 sorties were flown per day, totalling 310 flying hours in only seven days. On 4 May 1945, 39 Squadron flew its last Marauder operation when 12 aircraft bombed Popavaca; this was not only the finale for 39 Squadron but it is believed to be the very last operation flown by any B-26 during World War II.

By late 1945, the unit was in the Sudan and, by early 1946, the Mosquito B.VI and FB.26 also served alongside the Marauders. On 8 September 1946, 39 Squadron was disbanded at Khartoum, bringing an end to the Marauder's career with the RAF.

39 Squadron was the only other operational RAF unit to make good use of the Marauder from December 1944 through to late 1946. Note the hefty lump of armoured plate on which the 'winged bomb' is painted and the old desert camouflage, which indicates that this aircraft was once operated by 14 Squadron. (Via author)

THE RAID ON MELOS HARBOUR, 21 FEBRUARY 1943

E

By midday on 21 February, nine Marauders of 14 Squadron prepared to depart from Shalluffa. The RAF bombers headed north across the Mediterranean at just 50ft above the waves in a loose formation. The route took them through the Kaso Straits, east of Crete, before turning north-east towards Melos. As the Marauders approached the island, the attackers' plan began to unfold as the nine aircraft gathered into their three flights. 'A' Flight, led by Maj Lewis in FK370, accompanied by Fg Off R. W. Lapthorne in FK151 and Plt Off Clarke-Hall in FK142, prepared to lead the raid with a torpedo attack.

'B' Flight, led by Flt Lt E. Donovan in FK121 with Flt Sgt R. A. Barton in FK377 and Sgt B. H. Yarwood in FK139 broke away to port to begin their bombing run, which would take place on a northerly heading just 2 minutes after 'A' Flight's attack. 'C' Flight's Plt Off Phillips in FK123, accompanied by Flt Sgt G. C. Egebjerg in FK378 and Flt Sgt T. C. Bullock were ordered to break to starboard, circle around the island and then attack on a southerly heading 2 minutes after 'B' Flight had dropped their bombs.

'A' Flight reached the edge of the island and, after skimming a narrow strip of land east of Melos, dropped down to sea level on the southern edge of the harbour. Ahead were two merchant vessels and a coaster. Lewis chose the more southerly of the two merchant ships, which turned out to be the 1,300-ton *Artemis Pitta* which was laden with aviation fuel and military equipment. As Lewis jinked his bomber to line up on his target, Fg Off Lapthorne, on his port wing, was forced to quickly climb over Lewis's bomber before settling down on his starboard side to run a parallel attack on the same ship. Plt Off Clarke-Hall lined up on the second merchant vessel, the 1,700-ton *Thisbe*, which was only 200yd away from the *Artemis Pitta*.

As the final 800yds to the target point arrived, both Lewis and Lapthorne dropped their torpedoes. Only one found its target, causing a huge explosion in the stern of the vessel, which immediately caught fire due to its volatile cargo and began to sink. Up to this point, the enemy defences had been asleep but during Clarke-Hall's run the pretty tracer and unfriendly lumps of lead in between started to fill the air. Unfortunately, Clarke-Hall's torpedo did not find its mark and it is most likely that it actually passed under the hull of the *Thisbe*, which was unladen and high in the water. This was of no concern to Clarke-Hall, who set course behind his leader and colleague as 'A' Flight made its escape.

It was now 'B' Flight's turn and, despite a very short passage of time, 'A' Flight's attack had stirred up a hornet's nest and the defences were now ready. As Fg Off Donovan's flight approached the harbour in a line astern formation, they were greeted with a large pall of smoke covering the harbour from the burning *Artemis Pitta*. The crews at this point thought that several vessels were on fire and the untouched *Thisbe* was obscured by the smoke. It was also at this point that the flight realized that following a similar route into the harbour was not such a good plan as almost every available weapon suddenly opened up on them. The German defences had been recently bolstered by a battery of 88mm flak guns which added more weight to the established 20mm and 37mm guns all around the harbour.

All three Marauders took hits before they all attempted to get down to sea level and find a ship to attack. Low over the harbour, Sgt Yarwood's Marauder FK139 was never given the chance and was seen to rear up and explode before crashing very close to the *Thisbe*. Flt Sgt R. A. Barton's Marauder FK377 suffered a similar fate but in an attempt to gain height to allow his crew to escape, the bomber crashed into a cliff face near the entrance to the harbour.

Donovan's Marauder FK121 refused to be knocked out of the sky and, determined to attack at least one ship, he flew a half circuit of the harbour before lining up on the now-visible *Thisbe*. Pressing home his attack, Donovan dropped his load of four 500lb bombs onto the ship. The bombs overshot their mark as FK121 made its escape out of the harbour, managing to avoid soaking up any more of the German ground fire.

In contrast to 'B' Flight's experience, Plt Off Phillips led his three 'C' Flight Marauders in from the north and achieved complete surprise over the defenders. Once again sweeping low over the harbour, Phillips singled out the lone 700-ton coaster *Olympos* for his attack but unfortunately overshot his target. His wingmen plumbed for shore targets with Plt Off Egebjerg successfully hitting an enemy depot east of Adamas. Flt Sgt Bullock achieved similar success after planting his bombs into the harbour installations at Adamas. All three of 'C' Flight's Marauders escaped without any damage or injury to the crew.

Only 14 Squadron managed to achieve some success in using the Marauder as a torpedo bomber and photographs of the weapon in place are rare. On 21 February 1943, Maj E. Lewis SAAF led nine bombers in an attack against shipping in Melos harbour, sinking the 1,300-ton *Artemis Pitta*, which was laden with aviation fuel and military equipment. (Via 14 Sqn Association)

The South African Air Force

Thanks to its rapid expansion and deployment to North Africa, the SAAF was desperately in need of medium-level bombers. Large numbers of Marauder IIs were used to equip 12, 21, 24 and 30 Squadrons, SAAF under 3 Wing, SAAF and 25 Squadron would come under the control of the Balkan Air Force.

24 Squadron was the first of the South African units to convert to the Marauder in December 1943. The unit operated under 3 Wing, SAAF, until the end of the war but, from May 1945, the squadron's role changed from bombing to transport and all of its aircraft were stripped down for this purpose. Minus armament, these Marauders were the quickest military variants, with a cruising speed of 220mph at just 1,700rpm and they could carry a payload of 8,000lb. The Marauders carried out this tasking until the squadron disbanded in November 1945.

12 Squadron converted to the Marauder in January 1944 whilst serving in Italy. The unit supported the Allied advance all the way north until the Germans surrendered in May 1945. After a brief spell at Rivolto in northern Italy, the South Africans ferried their Marauders to Egypt in November 1945 and 12 Squadron was disbanded.

21 Squadron followed in July 1944 and had a similar career path to 12 Squadron, but disbanded in Egypt slightly earlier, in September 1945. 30 Squadron, which prior to its formation on 12 August 1944, was 223 Squadron, flew another Martin product, the Baltimore. Operating from Prescara, the squadron carried out its first Marauder operation on 20 August. From October, along with other squadrons in 3 Wing, the unit moved to Iesi and remained there until the end of the war. In peacetime, 30 Squadron swapped places with 39 Squadron at Biferno and, like 24 Squadron, finished its service in the transport role before disbandment came on 15 July 1945.

The last SAAF Marauder unit was 25 Squadron, which operated alongside 39 Squadron as part of the Balkan Air Force, attacking targets in Yugoslavia. Under the umbrella of 254 Light/Medium Bomb Wing, 25 Squadron saw a great deal of action and one of its aircraft, which was lost on the unit's last operation on 4 May 1945, infamously became the last Marauder to be lost in combat.

The Free French Air Force

The Free French Air Force began to receive the Marauder from late 1943 but its first aircraft were so war weary that it was not until March 1944 that the first official units were formed. Under the control of the 42nd Bomb Wing, Twelfth Air Force, the 31st and 34th Escadre (Esc) were formed, each comprised of three squadrons (Groupe de Bombardement), GBM 1/19 'Gascone', GBM 2/20 'Bretagne' and GBM 1/22 'Maroc' making up the 31st Esc and GBM 1/32 'Bourgogne', GBM 2/52 'Franche-Comte' and GBM 2/63 'Senegal' making up the 34th Esc. Both Escadre were not up to full strength until October 1944 but made a valuable contribution to the bombing effort until their last operation on 25 April 1945. All six Escadre were disbanded by June 1945 and all but three B-26s were returned to the USAAF whose crews flew them back to the United States for scrapping. The French Marauder units took part in 270 missions, made up of 4,884 combat sorties which saw 14 aircraft lost and 425 seriously battle damaged.

Two of the three aircraft that remained in France – B-26G 44-6188 named *Gaston Le Morvan* and 44-68219 – served as technical training airframes for military and later civilian apprentices. 44-68219 was saved from the axe and was donated by Air France to the Musee de l'Air at Le Bourget in 1964. Fully restored, the B-26 is on display today in its original Free French Air Force colours of GBM 2/20 'Bretagne'.

The third Marauder to remain in France was 43-4584, a B-26G-11-MA, which was converted by Dassault as a flying test-bed for the SNECMA Atar 101 turbojet. Re-registered as F-WBXM, the B-26 first flew in this configuration on 9 October 1950 and, following another change of registration to F-ZVLA, the aircraft was finally withdrawn from service on 14 May 1958.

The B-26 in the ETO and the Mediterranean

It was in the skies of Northern Europe that the B-26 was to find its true form, despite at first being sent like lambs to the slaughter in the low-level role. A rapid respect for the enemy's ground defences would see the bomber find its true niche as a medium-level specialist for the remainder of the war.

The Eighth Air Force and disaster over IJmuiden

Four B-26 groups were destined to join the Eighth Air Force in East Anglia under the control of the 3rd BW (Bombardment Wing) with its HQ at Elveden Hall. The first B-26 unit to arrive was the 319th BG, however, their stay was short and the group was transferred to North Africa in early November 1942.

By early December 1942, a second group, the 322nd BG, began to arrive. Ground personnel made Rattlesden and Bury St Edmunds their home and it was not until 7 March 1943 that the first B-26s arrived from the 450th BS. One month later, the 452nd BS followed and the 322nd BG began training for a method of flying that was alien to the Eighth Air Force.

The RAF had been flying low-level attacks throughout the war, while the philosophy of the Eighth Air Force was to maintain a high-altitude offensive. This offensive was flown by B-17s and B-24s, but having a medium bomber on the inventory opened up new possibilities. The RAF made good use of the Mosquito and Boston at low level while the medium Ventura and Mitchells were used against heavily defended targets at between 10,000 and 15,000ft. The Eighth Air Force was not enthusiastic but was prepared to look at using the B-26 for low-level operations where surprise and a good turn of speed

Shots of the 322nd BG in Eighth Air Force service are rare and this was taken not long after the group was transferred to the Ninth Air Force and moved to Andrews Field (ex-Great Saling). The 'PN' on the aircraft in the centre gives it away as belonging to the 449th BS. (Via author)

were essential. The sight of B-26s thundering low over the East Anglian countryside brought some locals out of the houses, while others shook their fists as they dived for cover in open fields. Brushes with trees and cables became commonplace and this was not helped by the control response of the B-26 which lagged an agonizing split-second behind the control input.

By mid-1943, the 322nd BG was deemed fit for operations and a 'baptism of fire' target was chosen, for a daylight attack on 14 May. Despite being located on the Dutch coast, the power station at IJmuiden, 10 miles north-west of Amsterdam, was by no means a cosy target. The RAF, having already attacked the plant on two previous occasions, had experienced a very warm reception from flak, thanks to an E-Boat station also being based there. It was now the turn of the USAAF, which detailed 12 B-26s, each carrying four 500lb delayed-fuse bombs, to attack the plant.

At 0950hrs on 14 May, the first B-26, flown by Maj O. Turner, CO (Commanding Officer) of the 450th BS, took off from Bury St Edmunds and set course for the Dutch coast, settling only a few feet above the waves to avoid German radar. Behind the formation, but still below radar, another B-26 with the 3rd BW commander, Brig Gen Brady and the group CO, Col Stillman of the 322nd BG, followed behind. Land was reached at Leiden, 20 miles south of the target, and a very alert gun crew quickly opened fire, damaging Lt R. C. Fry's aircraft, *Too Much of Texas*. The flak knocked out the port engine

A lovely shot, taken immediately after the engines had been shut down, of the pilot and co-pilot being informally debriefed about the operation. *Ginger*, a B-26B-20-MA 41-31767, belonged to the 449th BS, 322nd BG, and is displaying 19 mission symbols and six 'Duck' symbols, representing diversion missions. The bomber eventually succumbed to flak over northern France on 21 April 1944 but all six crew managed to bail out to become PoWs. (Via author)

and removed a large portion of the rudder as Fry turned his bomber away from the formation to jettison his bombs into the sea. Fry then settled down to concentrate on flying his damaged bomber more than 120 miles back to base on one engine.

The remaining bombers turned north followed a canal and railway track to IJmuiden where the air-raid siren went off at 1057hrs. Three minutes later, the formation was over the target and turning west for home after stirring up a hornet's nest of anti-aircraft fire. Meanwhile, Lt Fry managed to safely land at Great Ashfield while the mauled formation followed not long after. One B-26 put down at Honington while Lt J. J. Howell ordered his crew to bail out near Bury St Edmunds, leaving it to crash near Rougham. After regaining Bury St Edmunds, Maj G. C. Ceilo, the 452nd BS's commander, could not lower one of the undercarriage legs due to an enemy round. Ceilo circled the airfield for 80 minutes to build the hydraulic pressure back up before landing safely. Over 300 bullet holes were later recorded in Ceilo's B-26, but only one of his crew was wounded – he was one of just seven airmen injured on the whole raid, including Maj Turner himself.

A B-26B taxies to a halt at Andrews Field clearing displaying a healthy number of completed operations, which would become the type's heavily played-down trademark. (Via author)

Everyone who took part in the raid felt that they had done a good job but were not enthusiastic about repeating the exercise. The crews must have been stunned when, two days later, Col Stillman returned from a meeting at Elveden Hall, after being told that all of the bombs dropped on 14 May had missed their target. Stillman also received orders to attack the power station again on 17 May. Despite his protestations that it was too soon to fly another high-risk mission on the same target, he was overruled by Command, who stated that the operation was an integral part of operations all over Europe and it was too late to alter the target.

Late on 16 May, the order came through from Command for another 12 B-26s with the same bomb load. On this occasion, the force was to split into two on reaching the Dutch coast, with one group attacking another power station near Haarlem while the other would return to IJmuiden. With many aircraft still being patched up from the first raid, only 11 B-26s were declared serviceable for the mission which, this time, was led by Col Stillman.

From 1056hrs, the B-26s set course in bright sunshine again for the Dutch coast with all taking part, well aware that they would be pushing their luck to get home safely this time. Just over an hour later, a single B-26 returned early after being forced to turn back 30 miles from the enemy coast with a double generator failure. ETA for the remaining B-26s to land back at base was 1250hrs, but as this time came and went all those waiting at Bury, including Brig Gen Brady, were becoming increasingly uncomfortable with the potential outcome that no bombers would return that day. Once the 'all fuel exhausted' point had also passed, the optimists amongst the 322nd BG were hoping that their crews had diverted to airfields elsewhere in East Anglia. Unfortunately, this final hope was dashed when Command declared that the B-26s were listed as 'Missing in Action, cause unknown.'

A photo-reconnaissance sortie was flown that afternoon, which revealed that there was no evidence of bomb damage on either target. As the post mortem of the operation progressed, back at Bury St Edmunds it was discovered that the aborted B-26 might have been instrumental in the failure of the whole mission. Following the generator failure, the B-26 climbed to 1,000ft, which was standard operating procedure. However, in doing so the bomber had shown itself on RAF radar, which would mean that it had also appeared on German radar screens. Being 30 miles off the coast, this would have given the German defences plenty of time to prepare for the arrival of the 322nd BG. The story began to unfold further when a Royal Navy destroyer found two tired airmen in a dinghy several miles off the Suffolk coast. S/Sgt J. Lewis and S/Sgt G. Williams, rear and top turret gunners, were the only survivors of a B-26 that came down in the sea while attempting to get home.

Out of the 62 airmen who were forced down in enemy territory, 20 of them survived to become prisoners of war. Lt Col Purinton, who was the group executive officer and leader for the Haarlem attack, was rescued with his crew by a German boat. Incredibly, Col Stillman and two of his gunners were dragged from the remains of their B-26, alive but seriously injured.

In the meantime, a second unit, 323rd BG, had arrived at Horham on 12 May, destined to move to Earls Colne a month later. The 386th and 387th BGs arrived in June, settling at Boxted and Chipping Ongar respectively, giving the Eighth over 250 medium bombers at their disposal. Despite the mechanical problems that had been occurring, the 322nd BG's accident rate was no worse than that of any other groups. Another positive was that the last squadrons of the group to arrive and any subsequent groups were equipped with later production models with the bigger wing, larger tail surfaces, more fuel and many more improvements.

The Eighth Air Force commander, Gen I. C. Eaker, decided that the B-26s could add little weight to the USAAF's strategic bombing campaign in the ETO. All of the Marauder groups were placed under the Eighth Air Support Command (ASC), which was established to support ground forces – classed as a low-priority task within the Eighth Air Force. Reading between the lines, this may have been a subtle way of telling Washington that the B-26 was not cut out for operations in the ETO.

Taking note of how the Twelfth Air Force had been employing their B-26s in North Africa, the Eighth ASC considered the same tactic. The RAF was brought in to provide fighter cover with the B-26s flying tight formations of up to 18 aircraft at a height of 12,000ft, thus avoiding light flak. While the other groups continued to train at low levels, only Col Thatcher's 323rd BG were instructed to begin practicing the medium-level tactics. The D-8 bombsights slowly began to be replaced, and strike cameras and .50in machine guns firing downward from the ventral rear hatches were also fitted. Another two months had passed before the 323rd BG was ready for its first medium-level operation on 16 July 1943. The target was the marshalling yards at Abbeville. There were 18 aircraft that took part with a squadron of RAF Spitfires flying as escort. In all, 16 B-26s managed to drop their bombs while the formation endured heavy flak and the Spitfires drove off several enemy aircraft. The bombing was poor but all returned safely to Earls Colne. The decision had already been made to re-train the other three groups in the medium-level role.

A week later, the target was the Ghent coke ovens in Belgium, which escaped untouched but, on 26 July the airfield at St Omer/Longuenesse took

a pasting. The bombardiers were now getting the hang of their role, their accuracy was increasing and their escorts were enjoying high kill rates. The following day, during a raid on the airfield at Tricqueville, the Spitfires brought down nine Fw 190s for the loss of one aircraft, whose pilot was later rescued from the sea. Incredibly, the 323rd BG had flown nearly 100 sorties in five consecutive days over enemy territory without losing a single aircraft. The honeymoon period could not last, but it did show that the B-26 could survive operations when employed at the right height and with an escort.

During these early missions, the 322nd and 386th BGs had been flying diversions but from the end of July they also joined the fray. Neither had the same luck as the 323rd BG, especially on 30 July when, out of 21 aircraft dispatched to Woensdrecht airfield, only 11 managed to bomb and one 553rd BS B-26 was shot down. The 322nd was back in action on 31 July against Tricqueville. This time, rather than being nearly wiped out, one gunner, S/Sgt C. S. Maddox, claimed a Fw 190 shot down, which was confirmed by an escorting Spitfire pilot.

The bombing at this level, up to 3 August, had produced some indifferent results. On this day, the target was the Trait shipyards and 33 B-26s of the 322nd BG were dispatched. The raid went without a hitch, but the crews were unaware just how good it really was until strike photos were analyzed two days later. The shipyards were heavily damaged, and with the exception of just a few bombs, all had fallen within an area measuring 350×650yd. These results were not only encouraging for the crews but also for the senior staff who had their doubts about the B-26 even being in service, let alone becoming an

The 319th BG could boast many records, including the first B-26 to reach 50 missions – *Hell Cat*. It also had a host of aircraft that reached three figures including *ZERO-4* of the 437th BS, which is seen here displaying 150 mission symbols and five enemy air to air kills. Capt Richard C. Bushee (left) poses with his crew. (Via author)

effective combat aircraft. By the end of August, the B-26s had achieved the lowest loss-per-sortie rate of the entire Eighth Air Force. Having been the butt of many jokes, especially from B-17 crews, since their arrival, the B-26 had finally appeared to have silenced its critics.

Throughout September and early October, the Marauder groups had been successful against the airfield targets allocated to them and equally successful against enemy fighters. Using cloud to avoid the Spitfire escorts, the Luftwaffe struggled to knock the sturdy B-26s out of the sky and, during their Eighth Air Force service, 13 enemy fighters were claimed shot down by Marauder gunners. On 9 October, 1943, the 323rd and 387th BGs flew the last B-26 operation with the Eighth. In just three months, the reputation of this bomber was completely turned around and, after 90 medium-level raids made up of 4,000 sorties, only 13 B-26s were lost. Only one of these was brought down by an enemy fighter, which equated to a loss rate of just 0.3 per cent. On 16 October 1943, the four B-26 groups were transferred to the newly formed Ninth Air Force where they would go from strength to strength.

320th BG B-26C 42-107451 *Ann* lands back at Cognac having completed the group's 594th and last mission of World War II on 1 May 1945. (Via author)

The USAAF in the Mediterranean

The USAAF also had a presence in the Mediterranean when the 319th BG arrived in North Africa, after spending a few weeks under Eighth Air Force control in England. The group was transferred in November 1942, but what should have been a straightforward transit flight to St Leu in Algeria resulted in two B-26s being shot down over Cherbourg and a third crash-landing at Warmwell.

Now under the control of Twelfth Air Force, which was commanded by Gen J. H. Doolittle, the 319th BG was joined by the 17th BG in December and, by March 1943, the 320th BG was the third and final B-26 unit to operate in the theatre, all under the charge of the 42nd BW (MATAF, Mediterranean Allied Tactical Air Force). The 319th BG was the first to see action over Tunis on 20 December in support of Operation *Torch*. Doolittle wanted the B-26s to carry out their missions at 10,000ft following a spate of heavy losses during the early low-level raids against airfields, harbours and railway targets. The problem with the change of tactic revolved around the D-8 bombsight, which was designed for low-level operations and was very inaccurate at height. The solution was to introduce the Norden bombsight to a handful of B-26s,

One of the trademarks of the 319th BG was their six-abreast mass take-offs, here being demonstrated at Decimomannu in Sardinia. (Via author)

which acted as flight leaders on a raid, with the rest of the group bombing on their marks. Replacement aircraft were now being received with the Norden already fitted but it would still be several months before all of them were equipped with the higher-level sight.

Once the Germans and Italians were pushed out of North Africa, the B-26s went north in support of the Allies. Tactical bombing was still the order of the day but, once mainland Italy was invaded, the three groups had the Mediterranean to themselves, attacking various targets of opportunity. Like the RAF, the USAAF had its fair share of aerial kills as well, including many Ju 52/3ms and the Me 323.

It was with the 17th BG that the first B-26 reached 50 missions in spring 1943. *Hell Cat* reached this number while operating from Djedeida in Tunisia and, not long after, the aircraft, complete with its crew and crew chief were sent back to the US to take part in war bond tours.

Thanks to the nature of North African airfields, the 319th BG was the first unit to attempt six abreast take-off and landings in an effort to save time and fuel whilst forming up. The only problem was the dust and the practice was halted until the unit was moved to Decimomannu in Sardinia on 1 November 1943. Thanks to its 1,200ft-wide solid runway, complete with oiled-down take-off lanes, the big take-offs were back on. From here, the 319th BG continued to strike Axis targets throughout central Italy including important supporting roles at Cassino and Anzio. German lines were attacked in northern Italy throughout 1944 and, in March, the group earned a pair of Distinguished Unit Citations for superb attacks on marshalling yards in Florence and Rome. It also earned the Croix de Guerre for its support of the Allied forces as they advanced through Italy from April to June 1944. By August, the 319th BG was involved in the invasion of southern France, effectively hitting coastal defenses, radar installations and bridges.

By early 1945, the 319th BG were converting to the A-26, while the 17th and 320th BG continued on through France and, as the end of the war approached, briefly participated in raids on Germany as well. Already nicknamed *The Daddy of Them All*, the 17th BG, by then operating from Dijon, managed to achieve the highest number of combat missions of all B-26 units. On 1 May 1945, the 17th BG flew its last two missions, resulting in a grand total of 606 operations, made up of 13,041 sorties.

B-26B 41-31819 *Mild and Bitter* of the 452nd BS, 322nd BG, which was the first B-26 to reach the 50th-mission mark in January 1944 in the Ninth Air Force. This famous aircraft also managed to be first to reach the 100th-mission total. (Via author)

The Ninth Air Force

It was on 16 October 1943 that the Ninth Air Force was re-formed in England, after serving in the Mediterranean for 15 months. The Tactical Air Force immediately took charge of the Eighth Air Force's four B-26 bomber groups with over 225 aircraft on strength. While the Ninth Air Force would go from strength to strength, the B-26 groups at first represented the new organization's only striking force. Despite beginning to show its worth with the Eighth Air Force, the B-26 was also still viewed with some suspicion thanks to the earlier negative reputation it had gained. This was still difficult to shake off for those who had not flown the aircraft but for those who had, once mastered, the B-26 received nothing but praise from its crews.

The Ninth would continue to fly similar operations to those implemented by the Eighth Air Force and the first took place on 18 October when the 322nd BG was dispatched to bomb two airfields in France. Four days later, the six B-26s of the 322nd BG returned to the same target, but this was intercepted by at least 36 Bf 109Gs over Cambrai-Epinoy. Remarkably, despite the odds, the B-26 gunners not only managed to fend off the enemy fighters without loss, but also tentatively claimed three probable kills.

Fighter escort was reintroduced from 24 October when 36 B-26s were escorted, for the first time in the ETO, by a group of P-38 Lightnings. The B-26 crews appreciated the extra guns when another 40 enemy fighters launched themselves as the force approached Montdidier airfield. Once again, the enemy was fended off, even though the fighters made 54 passes on the bombers. This time, the gunners more confidently claimed three fighters destroyed, three probables and six damaged.

By November 1943, the Ninth Air Force had received double the number of B-26 groups on strength and, as a result, restructured the medium bombers into two combat wings. Each wing would contain two experienced groups and two new ones made up of the 98th Combat Wing (Medium) comprising the 323rd, 387th, 294th and 397th BGs and the 99th CBW made up of the 322nd, 344th, 386th and 391st BGs. None of the new groups were operational until February 1944.

Much of the B-26 group's time was initially taken up attacking Luftwaffe airfields which was part of the Eighth Air Force's *Pointblank* directive. However, only a few weeks after the Ninth Air Force was formed, RAF reconnaissance photographs began to reveal a new threat that would later emerge as the V1. The forthcoming invasion of Europe was already in the advanced planning stage by late 1943 and the discovery of this V-weapon had to be dealt with quickly. The Ninth Air Force now found itself participating in Operation *Crossbow*, which was designed to wipe out all of Hitler's V-weapons. The operations the B-26s would fly against the launching sites were known as *Noball* and the first attacks by B-26s began in late November 1943. The four operational bomb groups flew almost daily before the end of the year, racking up 1,790 successful sorties for the loss of just eight aircraft. In all, 30 aircraft had been lost by D-Day, however not a single V1 had been fired to disrupt the Allied invasion.

There was no science involved when applying invasion stripes; just a few chalked lines and nice big brush. An airman is seen preparing a B-26 of the 553rd BS, 386th BG, at Great Dunmow in early June 1944. (Via author)

The British obsession with the weather was soon understood and embraced by the Americans, who simply viewed it in terms of more scrubbed missions and a longer tour of duty in the ETO. Even once a mission set out, there was very often cloud over the target, which either resulted in a return for home or blind, often inaccurate, bombing. This problem was partly solved, from December 1943, through the donation of several *Oboe* Mk II sets from the RAF. These sets were fitted to several B-26s to form a new unit called the 1st Pathfinder Squadron (PS), which was under the leadership of ex-322nd BG, Maj R. A. Porter. The crews, who were all highly experienced, were drawn from the operational groups and the new squadron was activated at Andrews Field on 16 February 1944. Only five days later, the 1st PS was leading 17 B-26s of the 322nd BG on a raid on Coxyde airfield. Before the month was out, the 1st PS had swelled to 11 aircraft and 345 personnel.

In January 1944, the 322nd BG had cause for celebration, which was probably also toasted by the Martin Aircraft Company when one of their aircraft, B-26B 41-31819 *Mild and Bitter*, chalked up its 50th mission. Only

F

OPERATION *CROSSBOW* & THE 322nd BG

The B-26s of the Ninth Air Force operating from airfields in the east and south-east of England played a major role in Operation *Crossbow*. This long-term operation, which began in August 1943 and continued until the end of World War II, was tasked with the destruction and disruption of Germany's long-range weapons programme. At the time, this entailed the V1 flying bomb, the V2 ballistic missile and even the V3 supergun.

The 322nd BG, which arrived in England in December 1942 as part of the Eighth Air Force, was eventually transferred to the Ninth Air Force in October 1943. Under the command of Col Glenn C. Nye, the 322nd BG and its four squadrons, the 449th BS (PN), 450th BS (ER), 451st BS (SS) and 452nd BS (DR) made Andrews Field in Essex their home from 12 June, 1943. It was at Andrews Field that group began to be labelled as 'Nye's Annihilators', becoming very proficient at medium-level bombing following their first experiences in the ETO flying low-level operations for the Eighth Air Force.

By late 1943, the 322nd BG's role was now tactical and targets such as marshalling yards, bridges, road junctions and airfields were all on the agenda. It was *Noball* (codename for V1 sites) targets which were the greatest challenge though and operating alongside the RAF's 2 Group, of the 2nd TAF (Tactical Air Force), the 322nd BG successfully destroyed many V1 launching sites as part of Operation *Crossbow*.

Crossbow made up the majority of operations flown by the Ninth Air Force leading up to the D-Day invasion on 6 June, 1944. This came at a cost for the B-26s, 30 of them being brought down by flak during this period. Enemy fighters never played an active role against bombers attacking V1 sites.

While V1 sites were the most common targets, the previously mentioned V3 supergun or Hochdruckpumpe at Mimoyecques was attacked on at least one occasion by the 322nd BG. It was 5 November, 1943, when the partly constructed underground fortress was attacked for the first time by several B-26 bomb groups from the Ninth Air Force accompanied by 48 RAF Mitchells and 24 Bostons from 2 Group, 2nd TAF with fighter escort provided by 18 Spitfires from Fighter Command.

Poor weather forced the Boston element raid of the attack to turn for home, but the Mitchells, equipped with *Gee*, continued to the target in two waves leading in the B-26 groups. The crews at this stage had no idea of how important the target was, but the intensity of the flak on their arrival certainly made them realize that it was clearly worth defending. Several hundred 500lb bombs were dropped onto the fortress at Mimoyecques and while the RAF Mitchells managed to escape with only minor flak damage, two Ninth Air Force B-26s were not so lucky; one of them from the 322nd BG. This was B-26B-4, 41-8075 of the 452nd BS, *Impatient Virgin* flown by 1st Lt H. M. Price, the bomber being brought down by flak positioned at Landrethun-le-Nord, one mile west of Mimoyecques. The second and only other loss of the day was from the 386th BG operating from Great Dunmow. B-26B-30 41-31889 of the 553rd BS (AN) was shot down by flak 3 miles south-west of the target at Marquise; all six on board were killed.

six months prior to this, the air was blue with people calling for the B-26 to be removed from service and the thought of it actually achieving high mission rates was outlandish. In fact *Mild and Bitter* went one better and became the first B-26 to reach the even more magical 100th mission mark. After landing at Great Saling, following an attack on Evreux/Fauville airfield, the pilot Lt P. Shannon, who had flown *Mild and Bitter* 29 times, was immediately mobbed by personnel from Air Force publicity. Shannon was quoted as follows:

> All the flak missed us by a safe margin. *Mild and Bitter* has often been called the 'luckiest ship in the Ninth Air Force', having collected less than 50 flak holes, most of them small ones. Only once has battle damage kept her on the ground – a few days ago, when repairs on an electric line required about four hours, which wasn't enough time between missions. Her engines are the same ones that were first installed. Only a magneto change, a hydraulic pump and a few routine spark plug changes have been made. She has never made a one-engine return and never aborted a mission because of mechanical failure.

Shannon continued with what must have been a prepared statement.

> In her 100-mission career, *Mild and Bitter* has flown 449 hours and 30 minutes, 310 hours and 40 minutes of that in combat. She has travelled approximately 58,000 miles – more than twice around the world – and burned some 87,790 gallons of gasoline. She has carried 166 crewmen into battle, yet never has a casualty been suffered aboard her. Altogether she has hit military objectives in northern France 44 times, airfields 38 times and railway yards 14 times.

D-Day and 'the Bulge'

It was the C-47s of the Ninth Air Force that stole the limelight for the D-Day operation but the B-26s were also in the thick of it. From 0517hrs onwards on 6 June 1944, small, tight formations of six B-26s began to attack a host of specific targets along the beachhead. Loaded with 100lb bombs fitted with instantaneous fuses, the bombers were kept in small groups, reducing the risk of a large amount of ordnance falling on friendly troops if the targets were missed. Poor weather conditions kept the bombing height down to about 3,500ft and, by 0700hrs, nearly 400 B-26s had attacked various coastal gun batteries along the beachheads. Keen not to miss the biggest operation of World War II, the majority of bombers were quickly turned around to carry out a second attack before the day was over. Once the day was over, the B-26 and A-20 mediums had carried out over 1,000 sorties which was nearly a quarter of all flown by the Ninth Air Force on the 'Longest Day'.

Operation *Cobra*, which involved the US 30th Infantry Division pushing out of St Lo, began on 24 July. The plan was for 580 Ninth Air Force mediums to bomb an area 1 mile deep and 5 miles wide in front of the advancing troops. Some bombs inevitably fell short, killing several Allied soldiers, but generally, *Cobra* was a success and, the following day, the American soldiers pushed forward to Avranches and eastwards to outflank the German forces. This was the first time the B-26 had been used in such close quarters with Allied troops and the commanders on the ground describing the mediums as 'a mixed blessing', preferring to use fighter-bombers for this kind of operation in future. It was still behind enemy lines where the B-26 would prove most useful, especially with regard to disrupting lines of communication; bridges were a particular specialty.

By August 1944, five B-26 groups were operating from airfields in northern France, thus reducing the flying time to targets. In total, 6,602 sorties were flown during August, virtually all of them against French targets, in an effort to help the Allies push onwards towards Belgium and ultimately Germany. By December 1944, Europe was in the grip of a punishing winter and the Allied offensive had reached the Rhine. Hitler immediately took advantage of the situation, launching a final 500 panzer-strong offensive on 16 December that successfully pushed the thin American lines rapidly back to Malmedy and Bastogne. It was not until 23 December that mediums could respond in slightly clearer skies, armed with the knowledge that their bombing raids were vital to the survival of thousands of Allied troops on the ground. Once again, bridges were clinically destroyed along five supply routes that the Germans had exploited.

In all, 624 B-26 and A-20 sorties had been flown before the day was over and Allied fighter units were struggling to provide escorts for so many bombers. Up to this period, the B-26s had escaped serious attention from the Luftwaffe and several crews had not even seen an enemy fighter. This day though, the enemy fighters were out in force and, during the afternoon of 23 December, the pilots of IV./JG 3, flying the cannon-armed Fw 190A-8, claimed 27 B-26 kills in just nine minutes. Once the day was over, 35 B-26s had been lost, and, also thanks to accurate enemy flak, 182 bombers had been damaged to one degree or another. From now on, it was not unusual for an average of 50 to 60 Fw 190s or Bf 109s to attack the mediums. Regardless, the crews pressed on and, by mid-January 1945, the enemy was on the back foot. This was also a time when the Ninth Air Force was beginning to achieve some impressive records, including breaching 80,000 sorties and 100,000 tons of bombs dropped. Despite these alarming loss rates, the B-26's role in the ultimate defeat of the German forces in the Ardennes was crucial.

44-68221 started its flying career as a standard B-26G but was later modified into the one and only XB-26H. The aircraft was used to test the centreline undercarriage for the XB-48 and the B-47 which gained it the unflattering name of *The Middle River Stump Jumper*. (Via author)

CONCLUSION

An abrupt end

Once the Rhine was crossed, the B-26s continued to harry and destroy a host of tactical targets throughout Germany, continuing operations right up until the end of the war. Allied fighter cover became more prevalent but the brief and thankfully unexploited appearance of enemy jets during March and April kept the gunners on their toes. Only the 344th, 394th and 397th BGs remained active during the first few months of peace, while the rest were unceremoniously scrapped by the thousand. Even the surviving units only lasted until the end of 1945, by which time they had also joined the scrap heap. There was obviously no need, in peacetime, for aircraft like the B-26 and, along with the A-20 and P-51, large numbers were blown up and then melted down in Germany. Ironically, the very German industrial machine that the B-26s were trying to destroy only a few months earlier was being helped back to its feet by the metal that was being melted down from the Marauders. There was a similar process stateside, where a large disposal centre was set up at Walnut Ridge, Arkansas, and thousands of B-26s were flown directly there to be scrapped. Many Marauder veterans took this clinical end to their aircraft very personally while others just saw it as a step closer to getting home and away from the long and bloody war.

Despite the facts and figures that clearly gave the B-26 an excellent war record, it never fully shook off its poor reputation with senior staff. It was these armchair flyers who probably continued to rubbish the aircraft after the war, while the aircrew would continue to present a completely opposite and more accurate viewpoint. Regardless, the B-26 achieved a higher level of bombing accuracy than any other medium or high-altitude aircraft in the USAAF inventory and its longevity and durability gave the US taxpayer just as good, if not better value for money than many other aircraft built in the United States.

Luckily, not all B-26s were scrapped and it was thanks to Martin that the forward fuselage section of the most venerable B-26 of all was saved for posterity for the public to view at the Smithsonian, National Air and Space Museum in Washington D.C. *Flak Bait*, a B-26B, which served with the 449th BS, 322nd BG, broke all the averages to achieve 200 operations and, by the time the aircraft was retired, it had actually flown 207 operations. So the aircraft that the USAAF did not want, which was almost snuffed out of existence only days after World War II ended, is today preserved as the only surviving USAAF medium bomber with an extended war record. This is a fitting tribute to all the aircrew who were privileged to fly and fight in it and the ground crew who tirelessly kept the 'Much Maligned Marauder' flying.

BIBLIOGRAPHY & FURTHER READING

Birdsall, Steve & Greer, Don, *B-26 MARAUDER in action*, Squadron/Signal Publications (1981)

Freeman, Roger A., *B-26 MARAUDER at War*, Ian Allan Ltd (1977)

Freeman, Roger A., *Camouflage & Markings, B-26 Marauder*, Ducimus Books (1973)

Hamlin, John F., *Support and Strike!*, GMS (1991)

Jefford, Wg Cdr C. G. MBE, RAF, *RAF Squadrons*, Airlife (1988)

Johnsen, Frederick A., *Martin B-26 Marauder*, Specialty Press (2000)

Moore, Carl H., *Flying the B-26 Marauder over Europe*, TAB Books (1980)

Scutts, Jerry, *B-26 Marauder Units of the Eighth and Ninth Air Forces (Combat Aircraft 2)*, Osprey Publishing (1997)

Styling, Mark, *B-26 Marauder Units of the MTO (Combat Aircraft 73)*, Osprey Publishing (2008)

Wagner, Ray, *The Martin B-26B & C Marauder*, Profile Publications (1982)

INDEX